UNDERSTANDING TRENDS IN PROTESTANT EDUCATION IN THE TWENTIETH CENTURY

Compiled and Edited
by

Ronald H. Cram

University Press of America,® Inc.
Lanham • New York • Oxford

Copyright © 1998 by
University Press of America,® Inc.
4720 Boston Way
Lanham, Maryland 20706

12 Hid's Copse Rd.
Cummor Hill, Oxford OX2 9JJ

Library of Congress Cataloging-in-Publication Data

Understanding trends in Protestant education in the twentieth century
/ compiled and edited by Ronald H. Cram.
p.   cm.
Includes bibliographical references.
1. Christian education—History—Sources. I. Cram, Ronald Hugh.
BV1465.U53   1997   268'.804'0904 —DC21   97-44739 CIP

ISBN 0-7618-0987-2 (cloth: alk. ppr.)
ISBN 0-7618-0988-0 (pbk: alk. ppr.)

♾™ The paper used in this publication meets the minimum
requirements of American National Standard for information
Sciences—Permanence of Paper for Printed Library Materials,
ANSI Z39.48—1984

Dedicated to DCW

Contents

Preface   vii

Acknowledgements: xiii

Introduction:
Perennial Questions for
Education in the Christian Church   1
    Rhabanus Maurus   2
    Tatian   6

Starting Points: 11
    Darwin   12
    Spencer   15
    Bushnell   18

Starting Points: 25
    Dewey   26

The Rise of the Liberal Era: 32
    Coe   33
    Bower   40
    Chave   44
    Fahs   49
    Elliott   53

The Rise of the "Theological" Era: 57
    Smith   59
    Miller   66
    Sherrill   76
    Wyckoff   86
    Nelson   96

The Quest for Meaning: 109
    Philip Phenix   110

Recent Developments: 125
    JED   126
    Princeton's M.A. Syllabus   137

Index: 223

PREFACE

Protestant religious educators within the United States are plagued often by a loss of memory. Attempting to meet current and future needs, it is the rare religious educator who turns to the field's past for insight, challenge, or direction. Perhaps this is the result of the common sensical notions that new is better, and that the only thing we have to learn from the past is that it is out of date. Whatever the source(s) of history's lowly estate, religious educators frequently dismiss its importance all too quickly. True, there have been four overview of trends in religious education published since 1970: Wayne Rood's secondary source, UNDERSTANDING CHRISTIAN EDUCATION (1970); Harold Burgess' secondary source, AN INVITATION TO RELIGIOUS EDUCATION (1975); a collection of primary articles taken from the journal RELIGIOUS EDUCATION, and edited by John Westerhoff as WHO ARE WE? THE QUEST FOR A RELIGIOUS EDUCATION (1978), and Mary C. Boys' secondary source, EDUCATING IN FAITH: MAPS AND VISIONS (1989). Yet, the three secondary sources lack necessary primary readings that would enable the reader to enter into the historical process in a mature fashion, and the valuable book by Westerhoff (one of religious education's finest historians) is limited by its lack of materials before the twentieth century. The result is that some readers may conclude erroneously that people such as Coe or Bower came up with their ideas "on their own."

In a splendid interview by John Westerhoff of Lawrence Cremin in 1971, Westerhoff began:

> I've just finished reading the 688 pages of the first volume of your three-volume work on the history of American education. I plan to recommend it to everyone I meet, but I can just hear some of them saying, "That's an awful lot of reading. Why study history anyway?"

Cremin responded:

> You know the answers usually given: You study history
> to find out how we got the way we are or to avoid the
> mistakes of the past. But like most proverbial wisdom,
> the advice can be contradictory. Some say, "Those who
> forget history are condemned to repeat it," while others
> argue, "There is only one thing we learn from history and
> that is that men never learn from history." I have another
> notion. The historical mode is the characteristic Western
> way of understanding the world. Every propagandist
> knows this. All deliberate and unintentional myth-makers
> use history to support their myths. History is always
> being written and told for good and bad purposes by men
> seeking to influence their contemporaries in one direction
> or the other. Therefore, a prudent society must support
> the systematic study of its own history to protect itself
> from those who would use history for their own benefit.[1]

In an age where the question of meaning (and lack thereof) may be
yielding to (or mingling with?) the question of power (and the lack thereof)[2],
the role of history generally and the role of religious education in particular
must be called into question. Simone Weil once wrote that "the idea of
man's [sic] having death for a future is abhorrent to nature." She continued
to suggest that within this violent context, "to be outside a situation so
violent as this is to find it inconceivable; to be inside it is to be unable to
conceive its end. Consequently, nobody does anything to bring this end
about. In the presence of an armed enemy, what hand can relinquish its
weapon? The mind ought to find a way out, but the mind has lost all
capacity to so much as look outward.[3]

Parker Palmer, a major figure in current religious education theory has
echoed this feeling of powerlessness upon viewing a film that described the
construction of the first nuclear bomb, The Day After Trinity:

> I...saw, projected on a very large screen, the violence wrought
> by this way of knowing and living. In my own life, the
> dimensions of that violence eventually became clear. I was
> distanced and alienated from the world around me; too many
> parts of it became pawns in my game, valued only for how
> they might help me win. I worked toward shaping that world
> in my own image. Sometimes I succeeded--but the results
> were only temporarily pleasing, since the image in which I
> was shaping things was that of a distorted, driven self.
> Sometimes I failed, since the world does not always yield--

then the results were anger and even more violent efforts at compelling the world to change. The ultimate outcome for me was growing weariness, withdrawal, and cynicism. What else could result from a way of knowing and living driven mainly by the need for power and deficient in the capacity to love?[4]

History is one way of critically and positively responding to the growing feelings of alienation and powerlessness that plague the current American scene. History, as Cremin reminds us, is a way of influencing our contemporaries. For the religious educator, history may be viewed as an activity of hope. For without a vision of the future, there can be no history. In this context, history, its study and creation, is essentially a disciplined activity of the imagination--an artistic act, a prayerful act, an interpretive act of faith. Hayden White has written that the historical narrative

reveals to us a world that is putatively "finished," done with, over, and yet not dissolved, not falling apart. In this world, reality wears the mask of a meaning, the completeness and fullness of which we can only imagine, never experience. Insofar as historical stories can be completed, can be given narrative closure, can be shown to have had a plot all along, they give to reality the odor of the ideal. This is why the plot of a historical narrative is always an embarrassment and has to presented as "found" in the events rather than put there by narrative techniques.[5]

Though an "embarrassment," the manner by which the plot of religious educational history is conceived in our day is worthy of our boldest attention. This embarrassment, in fact, may be the most prized possession of the religious educator. For by taking history seriously, the religious educator proclaims a future in the face of an overwhelmingly dominant cultural acceptance of futurelessness.

The following text has three major purposes: 1) To introduce the reader unfamiliar with the development of central ideas in the history of twentieth century Protestant religious educational theory to primary representative selections from leading figures in the religious educational field; 2) To help the reader reflect on her or his own understanding of the purpose of religious education in light of historical precedents, specifically in the rise of twentieth century American Protestant religious education al theory; 3) To challenge the reader to engage in further historical research on his or her own. An assumption has been made that in order to better understand trends in twentieth century religious education, historical background is useful. Representative selections from the ancient church, then, will help frame certain basic and perennial questions education and religion raise when in dialogue. Representative selections from nineteenth and early twentieth century sources are offered in order to illuminate the manner in which certain basic and perennial educational questions were shaped and formed from within and without the Protestant educational context.

The format of the book is a simple one. Introductory paragraphs of explanation will precede primary reading that focus on foundational issues related to the rise of religious education theory in the twentieth century. Robert Ulich's Three Thousand Years of Educational Wisdom acted as a foundational format model. Ulrich's book, incidentally, makes a splendid companion volume to this current text.

The primary selections (most of which are out of print and difficult to find) may at first appear to be arbitrary. On the contrary, they have been carefully chosen in order to present a particular point of view regarding the rise of American Protestant religious education in the twentieth century. Many other selections could have been included, but those chosen seemed most representative for the ideas at hand. It is hoped that these selections will be used by the reader as invitations for the reading of full primary texts. The choice of selections, the inherent plot, and the accompanying commentary should provide ample opportunities for constructive debate regarding historical method and interpretation. Inclusive language has been used in my own commentary texts, but non-inclusive language has been left in original texts. The lack of inclusivity will often tell us something important about the era of scholarship under examination.

My thanks to all those students in the course I taught at Presbyterian School of Christian Education, The History of Religious Education in the Twentieth Century, for urging me to develop this book. Thanks also for Dr. James Hudnut-Beumler, Dean of Faculty at Columbia Theological Seminary, for his special support in the completion process of this book.

Ronald H. Cram
Decatur, Georgia
November, 1997

Notes

[1] Freeing Ourselves from the Mythmakers," John Westerhoff interviews Lawrence Cremin. <u>Colloquy</u>. July-August 1971, V.4. #7, pp. 7-8. Emphasis mine.

[2] See Thomas H. Olbricht, "Intellectual Ferment and Instruction in the Scriptures: The Bible in Higher Education," in <u>The Bible in American Education,</u> ed. David L. Barr and Nicholas Piediscalzi (Philadelphia: Fortress Press, 1982), pp. 97-119 for a thought provoking article along these lines.

[3] Simone Weil, <u>The Iliad or the Poem of Force</u> (Wallingford, Pa: Pendle Hill, 1983), p. 22.

[4] <u>To Know As We Are Known: A Spirituality of Education</u> (New York: Harper & Row, Publishers, 1983), p. 4.

[5] Hayden White, "The Value of Narrativity in the Representation of Reality," in <u>On Narrative,</u> ed. W.J.T. Mitchell (Chicago: The University of Chicago Press, 1981), p. 20.

ACKNOWLEDGEMENTS

Publishers and authors have permitted the use of copyrighted material:

Reprinted with permission of Simon & Schuster from CAN RELIGIOUS EDUCATION BE CHRISTIAN by Harrison S. Elliot. Copyright 1940 by Macmillan Publishing Company; Copyright renewed 1968.

Reprinted with permission of Simon & Schuster from THE GIFT OF POWER by Lewis Sherrill. Copyright 1955 by Macmillan Publishing Company; Copyright renewed 1983.

Reprinted with permission of Simon & Schuster from DEMOCRACY AND EDUCATION by John Dewey. Copyright 1916 by Macmillan Publishing Company, renewed 1944 by John Dewey.

Reprinted with permission of Scribner, a Division of Simon & Schuster from FAITH AND CULTURE by H. Shelton Smith. Copyright 1941 by H. Shelton Smith; Copyright renewed 1969.

Reprinted with permission of Scribner, a Division of Simon & Schuster from THE CLUE TO CHRISTIAN EDUCATION by Randolph Crump Miller. Copyright 1950 by Charles Scribner's Sons; Copyright renewed 1978.

Reprinted with permsiion of Scribner, a Division of Simon & Schuster from THE CURRICULUM OF RELIGIOUS EDUCATION by William Clayton Bower. Copyright 1925 by Charles Scribner's Sons, renewed 1953.

Reprinted by permission from the author, Philip Phenix,
REALMS OF MEANING: A PHILOSOPHY OF
THE CURRICULUM FOR GENERAL
EDUCATION, McGraw-Hill Publishing Company,
1964.

Reprinted by permission of James N. Lapsley, Princeton
Theological Seminary, "A Syllabus for Candidates for
the degree of Master of Arts, preparatory for the
Professional Examination (1983), pp. 1--10."

Reprinted by permission of Joseph H. Bragg, Jr., DOING
CHURCH EDUCATION TOGETHER: WHY AND
HOW JED WORKS, Joint Educational Development,
1978.

Introduction

Perennial Questions for Education in the Christian Church

With Two Sample Alternative Answers from the Early Church

The history of Protestant religious education in twentieth century America did not appear *ex nihilo*. There were centuries of preparation, experimentation, and criticism by the church of its educational rationales that inform (knowingly and unknowingly) its twentieth century theory and practice. Yet at the core of the church's educational theory and practice, three persistent and basic questions have been addressed perennially by religious educators either overtly or covertly: 1) How does one come to know truth? 2) What is education? 3) How shall the learner assume personal and social responsibility in the world? These three questions, in turn, have been informed by some notion of progress or of development--the evaluative standard(s) for the third question.

Two selections from early church history may act as symbols of two divergent manners of answering the questions cited above. The first selection comes from Rhabanus Maurus, a contemporary of Charlemagne, who was born in Mainz (where he later became Archbishop) about 766 C.E. A student of Alcuin, and later the head of the monastic school at Fulda, Maurus was intimately aware of the

Greco-Roman understanding of the *trivium* and the *quadrivium* which together came to be known as the "seven liberal arts." His theological understanding of how one comes to know truth was partially grounded in the seven liberal arts--a starting point with significant educational and theological consequences. Selections from chapters 1-25 of Maurus' "Education of the Clergy" are reprinted from F. V. N. Painter's translation found in his *Great Pedagogical Essays: Plato to Spencer* (New York: American Book Company, 1905), pp. 159-68. Painter's paragraph numbers have been changed to correspond to the original chapter structure used by Maurus. The last selection (from chapter 26) is my own translation from the German of Maurus' text found in *Sammlung der Bedeutendsten Pädagogischen Schriften aus Alter und Neuer Zeit* edited by Schultz, Gansen, and Keller (Paderborn, 1890), pp. 139-40.

****

RHABANUS MAURUS
(8th Century C.E.)

Book 3, Chapter 1.

An ecclesiastical education should qualify the sacred office of the ministry for divine service. It is fitting that those who from an exalted station undertake the direction of the life of the Church, should acquire fullness of knowledge, and that they further should strive after rectitude of life and perfection of development. They should not be allowed to remain in ignorance about anything that appears beneficial for their own information or for the instruction of those entrusted to their care. Therefore they should endeavor to grasp and include in their knowledge the following things: An acquaintance with Holy Scripture, the unadulterated truth of history, the derivative modes of speech, the mystical sense of words, the advantages growing out of the separate branches of knowledge, the integrity of life that manifests itself in good morals, delicacy and good taste in oral discourse, penetration in the explanation of doctrine, the different kinds of medicine, and the various forms of disease. Any one to whom all this remains unknown, is not able to care for his own welfare, let alone that of others.

Chapter 2.

The foundation, the content, and the perfection of all wisdom is Holy Scripture, which has taken its origin from that unchangeable and eternal Wisdom, which streams from the mouth of the Most High, which was begotten before every other creature through the Holy Spirit, which is a light incessantly beaming from the words of Holy Scripture. And when anything else deserves the name of wisdom, it goes back in its origin to this one source of the wisdom of the Church. Every truth, which is discovered by any one, is recognized as true by the truth itself through the mediation of the truth; every good thing, which is in any way traced out, is recognized and determined as good by the good itself; all wisdom, which is brought to light by any one, is found to be wisdom by wisdom itself. And all that is found of truth and wisdom in the books of the philosophers of this world, dare be ascribed to nothing else than just to truth and wisdom; for it was not originally invented by those among whose utterances it is found; it has much rather been recognized as something present from eternity, so far as wisdom and truth, which bring illumination to all with their instruction, have granted the possibility of such recognition.

Chapter 4.

Above all it is necessary that he, who aims to attain the summit of wisdom, should be converted to the fear of the Lord, in order to know what the divine will bids us strive for and shun. The fear of the Lord fills us with the thought of our mortality and future death. With mortification of the flesh it nails, as it were, the movements of pride to the martyr cross of Christ. Then it is enjoined to be lowly in piety. Therefore we are not to raise any objection to the Holy Scriptures, either when we understand them and feel ourselves smitten by their words, or when we do not understand them, and give ourselves up to the thought that we can understand and grasp something better out of our own minds. We should remember that it is better and more conformable to truth, to believe what is written, even if the sense remains concealed from us, than to hold that for true which we are able to recognize by our own strength.

Chapter 18.

The first of the liberal arts is grammar, the second rhetoric, the third dialectic, the fourth arithmetic, the fifth geometry, the sixth music, the seventh astronomy.

Grammar takes its name from the written character, as the derivation of the word indicates. The definition of grammar is this: Grammar is the science which teaches us to explain the poets and historians; it is the art which qualifies us to write and speak correctly. Grammar is the source and foundation of the liberal arts. It should be taught in every Christian school, since the art of writing and speaking correctly is attained through it. How could one understand the sense of the spoken word or the meaning of letters and syllables, if one had not learned this before from grammar? How could one know about metrical feet, accent, and verses, if grammar had not given one knowledge of them? How should one learn to know the articulation of discourse, the advantages of figurative language, the laws of word formation, and the correct forms of words, if one had not familiarized himself with the art of grammar?

Chapter 19.

According to the statements of teachers, rhetoric is the art of using secular discourse effectively in the circumstances of daily life. From this definition rhetoric seems indeed to have reference merely to secular wisdom. Yet it is not foreign to ecclesiastical instruction. Whatever the preacher and herald of the divine law, in his instruction, brings forward in an eloquent and becoming manner; whatever in his written exposition he knows how to clothe in adequate and impressive language, he owes to his acquaintance with this art. Whoever at the proper time makes himself familiar with this art, and faithfully follows its rules in speaking and writing, needs not count it as something blameworthy.

Chapter 20.

Dialectic is the science of the understanding, which fits us for investigations and definitions, for explanations, and for distinguishing the true from the false. It is the science of sciences. It teaches how to teach others; it teaches learning itself; in it the reason marks and manifests itself according to its nature, efforts, and activities; it alone is capable of knowing; it not only will, but can lead others to knowledge; its conclusions lead us to an apprehension of our being and of our origin; through it we apprehend the origin and activity of the good, of Creator and creature; it teaches us to discover the truth and to unmask falsehood; it teaches us to draw conclusions; it shows us what is valid in argument and what is not; it teaches us to recognize what is contrary to the nature of things; it teaches us to distinguish in controversy the true, the probable, and the _wholly false; by means of this science we are able to investigate everything with penetration, to determine its nature with certainty, and to discuss it with circumspection.

Chapter 22.

Arithmetic is the science of pure extension determinable by number; it is the science of numbers. Writers on secular science assign it, under the head of mathematics, to the first place, because it does not presuppose any of the other departments. Music, geometry, and astronomy, on the contrary, need the help of arithmetic; without it they cannot arise or exist. . . Ignorance of numbers leaves many things unintelligible that are expressed in the Holy Scripture in a derivative sense or with a mystical meaning.

Chapter 23.

We now come to the discussion of geometry. It is an exposition of form proceeding from observation; . . . the Holy Trinity makes use of geometry in so far as it bestows manifold forms and images upon the creatures which up to the present day it has called into being, as in its adorable omnipotence it further determines the course of the stars, as it prescribes their course to the planets, and as it assigns to the fixed stars their unalterable position. For every excellent and well-ordered arrangement can be reduced to the special requirements of this science. . . .

Chapter 24.

Music is the science of time intervals as they are perceived in tones. This science is as eminent as it is useful. He who is a stranger to it is not able to fulfil the duties of an ecclesiastical office in a suitable manner. A proper delivery in reading and a lovely rendering of the Psalms in the church are regulated by a knowledge of this science . . . Even with the Christian religion music is most intimately united; thus it is possible that to him, who does not know even a little music, many things remain closed and hidden.

Chapter 25.

There remains yet astronomy which, as some one has said, is a weighty means of demonstration to the pious, and to the curious a grievous torment. . .Astronomy, of which we now speak, teaches the laws of the stellar world. The stars can take their place or carry out their motion only in the manner established by the Creator, unless by the will of the Creator a miraculous change takes place...

That part of astronomy, which is built up on the investigation of natural phenomena, in order to determine the course of the sun, of the moon, and stars, and to effect a proper reckoning of time, the Christian clergy should seek to learn with the utmost diligence, in order through the knowledge of laws brought to light and through the valid and convincing proof of the given means of evidence, to place themselves in a position, not only to determine the course of past years according to truth and reality, but also for further times to draw confident conclusions, and to fix the time of Easter and all other festivals and holy days, and to announce to the congregation the proper celebration of them.

Chapter 26.

Based on the foregoing analysis, it should be clear by now that I believe Christians ought to have a sound understanding of the seven liberal arts. A careful understanding of philosophical discussions of this kind would be in the Christian's own best self-interest. Why? It is at this point that I would like to turn my attention to some specific issues for clarification. Let us imagine that something within the works of the philosophers seems to express an idea that parallels a truth in our own Christian faith. What shall we do, ignore the idea because it does not come directly from our Scriptures? On the contrary, we should boldly take the idea from the philosophers, and use it to strengthen the Christian faith. The philosophers, after all, blindly stumbled upon this truth by accident. It does not rightfully belong to them. Indeed, truth--whatever its origin--is the legitimate possession of the Christian alone. Remember that the

Israelites did not find slavery to be the only repulsive thing in
Egypt. False gods, sacred vessels, and corrupt images made
of gold and silver were intentionally left behind in their
exodus out of Egypt.

* * * * * * * * * *

The second selection could not be more fully theologically or
educationally divorced from that of Maurus. Unlike Maurus, Tatian had
a more narrow understanding of truth and human ways of knowing. An
Assyrian convert to Christianity, and then a pupil of Justin Martyr,
Tatian took an uncompromising view of regarding transcendence and
culture. Embracer of Gnosticism, and founder of the ascetic sect of the
Encratities (the "self-controlled"), he left the church with a clear
approach to the question of truth. Writing in the second century C.E.,
the following selections are from a larger anti-hellenistic polemic,
"Address of Tatian to the Greeks," found in The Ante-Nicene Fathers,
Volume II, edited by the Reverend Alexander Roberts and James
Donaldson (New York: Charles Scribner's Sons, 1899), pp. 65-83.

* * * * * * * * * *

                              TATIAN
                          (2nd Century C.E.)

Chapter 1
Be not, O Greeks, so very hostilely disposed towards the
Barbarians, nor look with ill will on their opinions. For
which of your institutions has not been derived from the
Barbarians? The most eminent of the Telmessians invented
the art of divining by dreams; the Carians, that of
prognosticating by the stars; the Phrygians and the most
ancient Isaurians, augury by the flight of birds; the Cyprians,
the art of inspecting victims. To the Babylonians you owe
astronomy; to the Persians, magic; to the Egyptians,
geometry; to the Phoenicians, instruction by alphabetic
writing. Cease, then, to miscall these imitations inventions of
your own. Orpheus, again, taught you poetry and song; from
him, too, you learned the mysteries. The Tuscans taught you
the plastic art; from the annals of the Egyptians you learned

to write history; you acquired the art of playing the flute from Marsyas and Olympus,--these two rustic Phrygians constructed the harmony of the shepherd's pipe. The Tyrrhenians invented the trumpet; the Cyclopes, the smith's art; and a woman who was formerly a queen of the Persians, as Hellanicus tells us, the method of joining together epistolary tablets: her name was Atossa. Wherefore lay aside this conceit, and be not ever boasting of your elegance of diction; for, while you applaud yourselves, your own people will of course side with you. But it becomes a man of sense to wait for the testimony of others, and it becomes men to be of one accord also in the pronunciation of their language. But, as matters stand, to you alone it has happened not to speak alike even in common intercourse; for the way of speaking - among the Dorians is not the same as that of the inhabitants of Attica, nor do the Aeolians speak like the Ionians. And, since such a discrepancy exists where it ought not to be, I am at a loss whom to call a Greek. And, what is strangest of all, you hold in honour expressions not of native growth, and by the intermixture of barbaric words have made your language a medley. On this account we have renounced your wisdom, though I was once a great proficient in it; for, as the comic poet [Aristophanes, Ranae] says,--

These are gleaners' grapes and small talk,--

Twittering places of swallows, corrupters of art.

Yet those who eagerly pursue it shout lustily, and croak like so many ravens. You have, too, contrived the art of rhetoric to serve injustice and slander, selling the free power of your speech for hire, and often representing the same thing at one time as right, at another time as not good. The poetic art, again, you employ to describe battles, and the amours of the gods, and the corruption of the soul.

Chapter 2

What noble thing have you produced by your pursuit of philosophy? Who of your most eminent men has been free from vain boasting? Diogenes, who made such a parade of his independence with his tub, was seized with a bowel complaint through eating a raw polypus, and so lost his life by gluttony. Aristippus, walking about in a purple robe, led a profligate life, in accordance with his professed opinions. Plato, a philosopher, was sold by Dionysius for his gormandizing propensities. And Aristotle, who absurdly placed a limit to Providence and made happiness to consist in the things which give pleasure, quite contrary to his duty as a perception flattered Alexander, forgetful that he was but a youth; and he, showing how well he had learned the lessons of his master, because his friend would not worship him shut him up and carried him about like a bear or a leopard. He in fact obeyed strictly the precepts of his teacher in displaying manliness and courage by feasting, and transfixing with his spear his intimate and most beloved friend, and then, under a semblance of grief, weeping and starving himself, that he might not incur the hatred of his friends. I could laugh at those also who in the present day adhere to his tenets,-- people who say that sublunary things are not under the care of Providence; and so, being nearer the earth than the moon, and below its orbit, they themselves look after what is thus left uncared for; and as for those who have neither bounty, nor wealth, nor bodily strength, nor high birth, they have no happiness, according to Aristotle. Let such men philosophize, for me!

Chapter 4

For what reason, men of Greece, do you wish to bring the civil powers, as in a pugilistic encounter, into collision with us? And, if I am not disposed to comply with the usages of some of them, why am -I to be abhorred as a vile miscreant? Does the sovereign order the payment of tribute, I am ready to render it. Does my master command me to act as a bondsman and to serve, I acknowledge the serfdom. Man is to be honoured as a fellow-man; God alone is to be feared,-- He who is not visible to human eyes, nor comes within the compass of human art. Only when I am commanded to deny Him, will I not obey, but will rather die than show myself false and ungrateful. Our God did not begin to be in time:

He alone is without beginning, and He Himself is the beginning of all things. God is a Spirit, not pervading matter, but the Maker of material spirits, and of the forms that are in matter; He is invisible, impalpable, being Himself the Father of both sensible and invisible things. Him we know from His creation, and apprehend His invisible power by His works. I refuse to adore that workmanship which He has made for our sakes. The sun and moon were made for us: how, then, can I adore my own servants? How can I speak of stocks and stones as gods? For the Spirit that pervades matter is inferior to the more divine spirit; and this, even when assimilated to the soul, is not to be honoured equally with the perfect God. Nor even ought the ineffable God to be presented with gifts; for He who is in want of nothing is not to be misrepresented by us as though He were indigent. But I will set forth our views more distinctly.

Chapter 5

God was in the beginning; but the beginning, we have been taught, is the power of the Logos. For the Lord of the universe, who is Himself the necessary ground of all being, insomuch as not creature was yet in existence, was alone; but inasmuch as He was all power, Himself the necessary ground of things visible and invisible, with Him were all things; with Him, by Logos-power the Logos Himself also, who was in Him, subsists.

Chapter 26

Cease to make a parade of sayings which you have derived from others, and to deck yourselves like the daw in borrowed plumes. If each state were to take away its contribution to your speech, your fallacies would lose their power. While inquiring what God is, you are ignorant of what is in yourselves; and, while staring all agape at the sky, you stumble into pitfalls. The reading of your books is like walking through a labyrinth, and their readers resemble the cask of the Danaids. Why do you divide time, saying that one part is past, and another present, and another future? For how can the future be passing when the present exists? As those who are sailing imagine in their ignorance, as the ship is borne along, that the hills are in motion, so you do not know that it is you who are passing along, but that time remains present as long as the Creator wills it to exist. Why am I called to account for uttering my opinions, and why are you in such haste to put them all down? Were not you born in the same manner as ourselves, and placed under the same government of the world? Why say that wisdom is with you alone, who have not another sun, nor other risings of the stars, nor a more distinguished origin, nor a death preferable to that of other men? The grammarians have been the beginning of this idle talk; and you who parcel out wisdom are cut off from the wisdom that is according to truth, and assign the names of the several parts to particular men; and you know not God, but in your fierce contentions destroy one another. And on this account you are all nothing worth. While you arrogate to yourselves the sole right of discussion, you discourse like the blind man with the deaf. Why do you handle the builder's tools without knowing how to build? Why do you busy yourselves with words, while you keep aloof from deeds, puffed up with praise, but case down by misfortunes? Your modes of acting are contrary to reason, for you make a pompous appearance in public, but hide your teaching in corners. Finding you to be such men as these, we have abandoned you, and no longer concern ourselves with your tenets, but follow the word of God. Why, 0 man, do you set the letters of the alphabet at war with one another? Why do you, as in a boxing match, make their sounds clash together with your mincing Attic way of speaking, whereas you ought to speak more according to nature? For if you adopt the Attic dialect though not an Athenian, pray why do you not speak like the Dorians? How is it that one appears to you more rugged, the other more pleasant for intercourse?

Chapter 29

Wherefore, having seen these things, and moreover also having been admitted to the mysteries, and having everywhere examined the religious rites performed by the effeminate and the pathic, and having found among the Romans their Latiarian Jupiter delighting in human gore and the blood of slaughtered men, and Artemis not far from the great city sanctioning acts of the same kind, and one demon here and another there instigating to the perpetration of evil,- -retiring by myself, I sought how I might be able to discover the truth. And, while I was giving my most earnest attention to the matter, I happened to meet with certain barbaric writings, too old to be compared with the opinions of the Greeks, and too divine to be compared with their errors; and I was led to put faith in these by the unpretending cast of the language, the inartificial character of the writers, the foreknowledge displayed of future events, the excellent quality of the precepts, and the declaration of the government of the universe as centered in one Being. And, my soul being taught of God, I discern that the former class of writings lead to condemnation, but that these put an end to the slavery that is in the world, and rescue us from a multiplicity of rulers and ten thousand tyrants, while they give us, not indeed what we had not before received, but what we had received but were prevented by error from retaining.

Chapter 30

Therefore, being initiated and instructed in these things, I wish to put away my former errors as the follies of childhood. For we know that the nature of wickedness is like that of the smallest seeds; since it has waxed strong from a small beginning, but will again be destroyed if we obey the words of God and do not scatter ourselves. For He has become master of all we have by means of a certain "hidden treasure," which while we are digging for we are indeed covered with dust, but we secure it as our fixed possession. He who receives the whole of this treasure has obtained command of the most precious wealth. Let these things, then, be said to our friends. But to you Greeks what can I say, except to request you not to rail at those who are better than yourselves, nor if they are called Barbarians to make that an occasion of banter? For, if you are willing, you will be able to find our the cause of men's not being able to understand one another's language; for to those who wish to examine our principles I will give a simple and copious account of them.

Chapter 42

These things, O Greeks, I Tatian, a disciple of the barbarian philosophy, have composed for you. I was born in the land of the Assyrians, having been first instructed in your doctrines, and afterwards in those which I now undertake to proclaim. Henceforward, knowing who God is and what is His work, I present myself to you prepared for an examination concerning my doctrines, while I adhere immoveably to that mode of life which is according to God.

* * * * * * * * * *

As the following selections are studied, the reader is encouraged to reflect back on the writings of Maurus and Tatian. For the issues raised by these two early Christian writers with regard to truth, education, the assumption of personal and social responsibility and progress have educational and theological variants to the present day in American Protestant religious education theory and practice.

Starting Points

Darwin, Spencer, Bushnell

The traditional starting point chosen to begin thinking about Protestant religious education in twentieth century America is Horace Bushnell. While it cannot be denied that Bushnell is a central figure in the rise of contemporary religious education, a more pervasive influence must be considered. While Bushnell was important, it was Charles Darwin who indirectly shaped the church's educational enterprise more than anyone else during the first fifty years of the twentieth century.

Born in Shrewsbury, England in 1809, Darwin was to become a student of medicine, a student of biology, a student of theology, and one of three major shapers of twentieth century thought in the West (the other two being Marx and Freud). Darwin saw the world as a place governed by laws. The eventual development of a theory of artificial selection and natural selection through the struggle for existence was cast in positive progressive terms. His evolutionary theory soon came to be applied not only to the biological world, but to such areas as economics, sociology, psychology, theology, philosophy, history, *and* education. The latter was specifically addressed by the philosopher Herbert Spencer, a close friend of Darwin. The usefulness of biological models and metaphors in describing the symbolic world is, at the very least, problematic. But the inherent ideas of progress and competition introduced by Darwin took root in American soil and prospered. These ideas entered into twentieth century American Protestant religious education by osmosis, and dramatically shaped its history.

Add to this *ethos* of natural selection the child-centered progressive enculturation model of Bushnell (primarily informed by continental Romanticism), and the resulting image is one that fit the early twentieth century industrial American context like a glove. The following readings from Darwin (1859), Spencer (1860), and Bushnell (1861) provide some windows into the dynamic issues at stake from the very beginning of the modern Protestant American religious education movement.

* * * * * * * * * *

Charles Darwin
(1859)

[From *The Origin of Species by Means of Natural Selection or The Preservation of Favored Races in the Struggle for Life and The Descent of Man and Selection in Relation to Sex* (New York: The Modern Library, 1936), pp. 63-4, 373-74. These selections are taken from the *Origin*.]

How will the struggle for existence, briefly discussed in the last chapter, act in regard to variation? Can the principle of selection, which we have seen is so potent in the hands of man, apply under nature? I think we shall see that it can act most efficiently. Let the endless number of slight variations and individual differences occurring in our domestic productions, and, in a lesser degree, in those under nature, be borne in mind; as well as the strength of the hereditary tendency. Under domestication, it may be truly said that the whole organisation becomes in some degree plastic. But the variability, which we almost universally meet with in our domestic productions, is not directly produced, as Hooker and Asa Gray have well remarked, by man; he can neither originate varieties, nor prevent their occurrence; he can preserve and accumulate such as do occur. Unintentionally he exposes organic beings to new and changing conditions of life, and variability ensues; but similar changes of conditions might and do occur under nature. Let it also be borne in mind how infinitely complex and close-fitting are the mutual relations of all organic beings to each other and to their physical conditions of life; and consequently what infinitely varied diversities of structure might be of use to each being under changing conditions of life. Can it, then, be thought improbable, seeing that variations useful to man have undoubtedly occurred, that other variations useful in some way to each being in the great and complex battle of life, should occur in the course of many successive generations. If such do-occur, can we doubt (remembering that many more individuals are born than can possibly survive) that individuals having any advantage, however slight, over others, would have the best chance of surviving and or procreating their kind? On the other hand, we may feel sure that any variation in the least degree injurious would be rigidly destroyed. This preservation of favourable individual differences and variations, and the destruction of those which are injurious, I have called Natural Selection, or the Survival of the Fittest. Variations neither useful nor injurious would not be affected by natural selection, and would be left either a fluctuating element, as perhaps we see in certain polymorphic species, or would ultimately become fixed, owing to the nature of the organism and the nature of the conditions.

Several writers have misapprehended or objected to the term Natural Selection. Some have even imagined that natural selection induced variability, whereas it implies only the preservation of such variations as arise and are beneficial to the being under its conditions of life. No one objects to agriculturists speaking of the potent effects of man's selection; and in this case the individual differences given by nature, which man for some object selects, must of necessity first occur. Others have objected that the term selection implies conscious choice in the animals which become modified; and it has even been urged that, as plants have no volition, natural selection is not applicable to them! In the literal sense of the word, no doubt, natural selection is a false term; but who ever objected to chemists speaking of the elective affinities of the various elements?--and yet an acid cannot strictly be said to elect the base with which it in preference combines. It has been said that I speak of natural selection as an active power or Deity; but who objects to an author speaking of the attraction of gravity as ruling the movements of the planets? Every one knows what is meant and is implied by such metaphorical expressions; and they are almost necessary for brevity. So again it is difficult to avoid personifying the word Nature; but I mean by Nature, only the aggregate action and product of many natural laws, and by laws the sequence of events as ascertained by us. With a little familiarity such superficial objections will be forgotten. . . .

In the future I see open fields for far more important researches. Psychology will be securely based on the foundation already well laid by Mr. Herbert Spencer, that of the necessary acquirement of each mental power and capacity by graduation. Much light will be thrown on the origin of man and his history.

Authors of the highest eminence seem to be fully satisfied with the view that each species has been independently created. To my mind it accords better with what we know of the laws impressed on matter by the Creator, that the production and extinction of the past and present inhabitants of the world should have been due to secondary causes, like those determining the birth and death of the individual. When I view all beings not as special creations, but as the lineal descendants of some few beings which lived long before the first bed of the Cambrian system was deposited, they seem to me to become ennobled. Judging from the past, we may safely infer that not one living species will transmit its unaltered likeness to a distant futurity. And of the species now living very few will transmit progeny of any kind to a far distant futurity; for the manner in which all organic beings are grouped, shows that the greater number of species in each genus, and all the species in many genera, have left no descendants, but have become utterly extinct. We can so far take a prophetic glance into futurity as to foretell that it will be the common and widely-spread species, belonging to the larger and dominant groups within each class, which will ultimately prevail and procreate new and dominant species.

As all the living forms of life are the lineal descendants of those which lived long before the Cambrian epoch, we may feel certain that the ordinary succession by generation has never once been broken, and that no cataclysm has desolated the whole world. Hence we may look with some confidence to a secure future of great length. And as natural selection works solely by and for the good of each being, all corporeal and mental endowments will tend to progress towards perfection.

It is interesting to contemplate a tangled bank, clothed with many plants of many kinds, with birds singing on the bushes, with various insects flitting about, and with worms crawling through the damp earth, and to reflect that these elaborately constructed forms, so different from each other, and dependent upon each other in so complex a manner, have all been produced by laws acting around us. These laws, taken in the largest sense, being Growth with Reproduction; Inheritance which is almost imipolied by reproduction; Variability from the indirect and direct action of the conditions of life, and from use and disuse; a Ratio of Increase so high as to lead to a Struggle for Life, and as a consequence to Natural Selection, entailing Divergence of Character and the Extinction of less-improved forms. Thus, from the war of nature, from famine and death, the most exalted object which we are capable of conceiving, namely, the production of the higher animals, directly follows. There is grandeur in this view of life, with its several powers, having been originally breathed by the Creator into a few forms or into one; and that, whilst this planet has gone cycling on according to the fixed law of gravity, from so simple a beginning endless forms most beautiful and most wonderful have been, and are being evolved.

* * * * * * * * * *

Herbert Spencer
(1860)

[From *Education: Intellectual, Moral, and Physical* (New York: D. Appleton and Company, 1860), pp. 162-71.]

Strangely enough, the most glaring defect in our programmes of education is entirely-overlooked. While much is being done in the detailed improvement of our systems in respect both of matter and manner, the most pressing desideratum has not yet been even recognised as a desideratum. To prepare the young for the duties of life is tacitly admitted by all to be the end which parents and schoolmasters should have in view; and happily the value of the things taught, and the goodness of the method followed in teaching them, are now ostensibly judged by their fitness to this end. The propriety of substituting for an exclusively classical training a training in which the modern languages shall have a share, is argued on this ground. The necessity of increasing the amount of science is urged for like reasons. But though some care is taken to fit youth of both sexes for society and citizenship, no care whatever is taken to fit them for the still more important position they will ultimately have to fill--the position of parents. While it is seen that for the purpose of gaining a livelihood, an elaborate preparation is needed, it appears to be thought that for the bringing up of children, no preparation whatever is needed. While many years are spent by a boy in gaining knowledge, of which the chief value is that it constitutes 'the education of a gentlemen;' and while many years are spent by a girl in those decorative acquirements which fit her for evening parties; not an hour is spent by either of them for that gravest of all responsibilities--the management of a family. Is it that each may be trusted by self-instruction to fit himself, or herself, for the office of parent? No: not only is the need for such self-instruction unrecognised, but the complexity of the subject renders it the one of all others in which self-instruction is least likely to succeed. No rational plea can be put forward for leaving the Art of Education out of our *curriculum.* Whether as bearing upon the happiness of parents themselves, or whether as affecting the characters and lives of their children and remote descendants, we must admit that a knowledge of the right methods of juvenile culture, physical, intellectual, and moral, is a knowledge second to none in importance. This topic should occupy the highest and last place in the course of instruction passed through by each man and woman. As physical maturity is marked by the ability to produce offspring, so mental maturity is marked by the ability to train those offspring. *The subject which involves all other subjects, and therefore the subject in which the education of every one should culminate, is the Theory and Practice of Education.*

In the absence of this preparation, the management of children, and more especially the moral management, is lamentably bad. Parents either never think about the matter at all, or else their conclusions are crude and inconsistent. In most cases, and especially on the part of mothers, the treatment adopted on every occasion is that which the impulse of the moment prompts: it springs not from any reasoned-out conviction as to what will most conduce to the child's welfare, but merely expresses the passing parental feelings, whether good or ill; and varies from hour to hour as these feelings vary. Or if these blind dictates of passion are supplemented by any definite doctrines and methods, they are those that have been handed down from the past, or those suggested by the remembrances of childhood, or those adopted from nurses and servants--methods devised not by the enlightenment, but by the ignorance of the time. . . .

We are not among those who believe in Lord Palmerston's dogma, that "all children are born good. On the whole, the opposite dogma, untenable as it is, seems to us less wide of the truth. Nor do we agree with those who think that, by skillful discipline, children may be made altogether what they should be. Contrariwise, we are satisfied that though imperfections of nature may be diminished by wise management, they cannot be removed by it. The notion that an ideal humanity might be forthwith produced by a perfect system of education, is near akin to that shadowed forth in the poems of Shelley, that would mankind give up their old institutions, prejudices, and errors, all the evils in the world would at once disappear: neither notion being acceptable to such as have dispassionately studied human affairs.

Not that we are without sympathy with those who entertain these too sanguine hopes. Enthusiasm, pushed even to fanaticism, is a useful motive-power--perhaps an indispensable one. It is clear that the ardent politician would never undergo the labours and make the sacrifices he does, did he not believe that the reform he fights for is the one thing needful. But for his conviction that drunkenness is the root of almost all social evils, the teetotaller would agitate far less energetically. In philanthropy as in other things great advantage results from division of labour; and that there may be division of labour, each class of philanthropists must be more or less subordinated to its function--must have an exaggerated faith in its work. Hence, of those who regard education, intellectual or moral, as the panacea, we may say that their undue expectations are not without use; and that perhaps it is part of the beneficent order of things that their confidence cannot be shaken.

Even were it true, however, that by some possible system of moral government children could be moulded into the desired form; and even could every parent be duly indoctrinated with this system; we should still be far from achieving the object in view. It is forgotten that the carrying out of any such system presupposes, on the part of adults, a degree of intelligence of goodness, of self-control, possessed by no one. The greatest error made by those who discuss questions of juvenile discipline, is in ascribing all the faults and difficulties to the children, and none to the parents. The current assumption respecting family government, as respecting national government, is, that the virtues are with the rulers and the vices with the ruled. Judging by educational theories, men and women are entirely transfigured in the domestic relation. The citizens we do business with, the people we meet in the world, we all know to be very imperfect creatures. In the daily scandals, in the quarrels of friends, in bankruptcy disclosures, in lawsuits, in police reports, we have constantly thrust before us the pervading selfishness, dishonesty, brutality. Yet when we criticise nursery management, and canvass the misbehaviour of juveniles, we habitually take for granted that these culpable men and women are free from moral delinquency in the treatment of their offspring! So far is this from the truth, that we do not hesitate to say that to parental misconduct is traceable a great part of the domestic disorder commonly ascribed to the perversity of children. We do not assert this of the more sympathetic and self-restrained, among whom we hope most of our readers may be classed, but we assert it of the mass. What kind of moral discipline is to be expected of a mother who, time after time, angrily shakes her infant because it will not suckle her, which we once saw a mother do? How much love of justice and generosity is likely to be instilled by a father who, on having his attention drawn by his child's scream to the fact that its finger is jammed between the window sash and the sill, forthwith begins to beat the child instead of releasing it? Yet that there are such fathers is testified to us by an eye-witness. Or, to take a still stronger case, also vouched for by direct testimony--what are the educational prospects of the boy who, on being taken home with a dislocated thigh, is saluted with a castigation? It is true that these are extreme instances--instances exhibiting in human beings that blind instinct which impels brutes to destroy the weakly and injured of their own race. But extreme though they are, they typify feelings an conduct daily observable in many families. Who has not repeatedly seen a child slapped by a nurse or parent for a fretfulness probably resulting from bodily derangement? Who, when watching a mother snatch up a fallen little one, has not often traced, both in the rough manner and in the sharply-uttered exclamation-- 'You stupid little thing!'--an irascibility foretelling endless future squabbles? Is there not in the harsh tones in which a father bids his children be quiet, evidence of a deficient fellow-feeling with them? Are not the constant, and often quite needless, thwartings that the young experience--the injunctions to sit still, which an active child cannot obey without suffering great nervous irritation, the commands not to look out of the window when travelling by railway, which on a child of any intelligence entails serious deprivation--are not these thwartings, we ask, signs of a terrible lack of sympathy?   The truth is, that the difficulties of moral education are necessarily of dual origin--necessarily result from the combined faults of parents and children.   If hereditary transmission is a law of nature, as every naturalist knows it to be, and as our daily remarks and current proverbs admit it to be; then on the average of cases, the defects of children mirror the defects of their parents;--on the average of cases, we say, because, complicated as the results are by the transmitted traits of remoter ancestors, the correspondence is not special, but only general.   And if, on the average of cases, this inheritance of defects exists, then the evil passions which parents have to check in their children imply like evil passions in themselves: hidden, it may be, from the public eye; or perhaps obscured by other feelings; but still there. Evidently, therefore, the general practice of any ideal system of discipline is hopeless: parents are not good enough.

* * * * * * * * *

Horace Bushnell

(1861)

[From *Christian Nurture* (New York: Charles Scribner's Sons, 1883), pp. 253-64.]

"For I know him, that he will command his children and his household after him, and they shall keep the way of the Lord."--Genesis, xviii. 19.

The real point of the declaration, here, is not that Abraham will command his children, but that he is such a man, having such qualities or qualifications as to be able to command, certain to command, and train them into an obedient and godly life. The declaration is, you will observe--"For I know *him*; not simply and directly--"For I know the fact." Every thing turns on what is *in him* as a father and householder--his qualifications, dispositions, principles, and modes of life--and the declaration is, that what he is to do, will certainly come out of what he is. He will certainly produce, or train a godly family, because it is in him, as a man, to do nothing else or less. The subject raised then by the declaration is, not so much family training and government, as it is--

The personal and religious qualifications, or qualifications of character, necessary to success in such family training and government.

There is almost no duty or work, in this world, that does not require some outfit of qualifications, in order to the doing of it well. We all understand that some kind of preparation is necessary to fill the place of a magistrate, teach a school, drill a troop of soldiers, or do any such thing, in a right manner. Nay, we admit the necessity of serving some kind of apprenticeship, in order to become duly qualified for the calling, only of a milliner, or a tailor. And yet, as a matter of fact, we go into what we call the Christian training of our children, without any preparation for it whatever, and apparently without any such conviction of negligence or absurdity, as at all disturbs our assurance in what we do. Not that young parents, and especially young mothers, are not often heard lamenting their conscious insufficiency for the charge that is put upon them, but that, in such regrets, they commonly mean nothing more than that they feel very tenderly, and want to do better things than, in fact, any body can. It does not mean, as a general thing, that they are practically endeavoring to get hold of such qualifications as they want, in order to their Christian success. After all, it is likely to be assumed that they have their sufficient equipment in the tender instinct of their natural affection itself. So they go on, as in a kind of venture, to command, govern, manage, punish, teach, and turn about the way of their child, in just such tempers, and ways of example and views of life, as chance to be the element of their own disfigures, ill-begotten character at the time. This, in short, is their sin--the undoing, as it will by and by appear, of their children--that they undertake their most sacred office, without any sacred qualifications; govern without self-government, discharge the holiest responsibilities irresponsibly, and thrust their children into evil, by the evil and bad mind, out of which their training proceeds.

I know not any thing that better shows the utter incompetency of mere natural affection as an equipment for the parental office, or that, in a short way, proves the fixed necessity in it, of some broader competency and higher qualification, than just to glance at the real cruelties, even commonly perpetrated, under just those tender, faithful instigations of natural affection, that we so readily expect to be a kind of infallible protection to the helplessness of infancy. How often is it a fact, that the fondest parents, owing to some want of insight, or of patience, or even to some uninstructed, only half intelligent desire to govern their child, will do it the greatest wrongs--stinging every day and hour, the little defenseless being, committed to their love, with the sense of bitter injustice; driving in the ploughshare of abuse and blame upon its tender feeling, by harsh words and pettish chastisements, when, in fact, the very thing in the child that annoys them is, that they themselves have thrown it into a fit of uneasiness and partial disorder, by their indiscreet feeding; or that in some appearance of irritability, or insubjection, it has only not the words to speak of its pain, or explain its innocence. The little child's element of existence becomes, in this manner, not seldom, an element of bitter wrong, and the sting of wounded justice grows in, so to speak, poisoning the soul all through, by its immedicable rancor. The pain of such wrong goes deeper, too, than many fancy. No other creature suffers under conscious injury so intensely. And the mischief done is only aggravated by the fact that the sufferer has not power of redress, and has no alternative permitted, but either to be cowed into a weak and cringing submission or else, when his nobler nature has too much stuff in it for that, to be stiffened in hate and the bitter grudges of wrong. I know not any thing more sad to think of, than the cruelties put upon children in this manner. It makes up a chapter which few persons read, and which almost every body takes for granted can not exist. For the honor of our human nature, I wish it could not; and that what we call maternal affection, the softest, dearest, most self-sacrificing of all earthly forms of tenderness and fidelity, were, at least, sufficient to save the dishonor, which, alas! it is not; for these wrongs are, in fact, the cruelties of motherhood, and as often, I may add, of an even over-fond motherhood, as any--wrongs of which the doers are unconscious, and which never get articulated, save by the sobbings of the little bosom, where the sting of injury is felt.

Here, then, at just the point where we should, least of all, look for it, viz: at the point of maternal affection itself, we have displayed, in sadly convincing evidence, the need and high significance of those better qualifications of mind and character, by which the training of children becomes properly Christian, and upon which, as being such, the success of that training depends. Few persons, I apprehend, have any conception, on the other hand, of the immense number and sweep of the disqualifications that, in nominally or even really Christian parents, go in to hinder, and spoil of all success, the religious nurture of their children. Sometimes the disqualification is this, and sometimes it is that; sometimes conscious, sometimes unconscious; sometimes observable by others and well understood, and sometimes undiscovered. The variety is infinite, and the modes of combination subtle, to such a degree, that persons taken to be eminently holy in their life, will have all their prayers and counsels blasted, by some hidden fatality, whose root is never known, or suspected, whether by others, or possibly by themselves. The wonder that children, whose parents were in high esteem for their piety, should so often grow up into a vicious and ungodly life, would, I think, give way to just the contrary wonder, if only some just conception were had of the various, multifarious, unknown, unsuspected disqualifications, by which modes of nurture, otherwise good, are fatally poisoned. Sometimes, for example, it is a fatal mischief, going before on the child, but probably unknown to the world, that the parents, one or both, or it may be the mother especially, does not accept the child willingly, but only submits to the maternal office and charge, as to some hard necessity. This charge is going to detain her at home, and limit her freedom. Or it will take her away from the shows and pleasure for which she is living. Or it will burden her days and nights with cares that weary her self-indulgence. Or she is not fond of children, and never means to be fond of them--they are not worth the trouble they cost. Indulging these and such like discontents, unwisely and even cruelly provoked, not unlikely, by the unchristian discontents and foolish speeches of her husband, she poisons both herself and her child beforehand, and receives it with no really glad welcome, when she takes it to her bosom. Strange mortal perversity that can thus repel, as a harsh intrusion, one of God's dearest gifts; that which is the date of the house in its coming, and comes to unseal a new passion, whereby life itself shall be duplicated in meaning, as in love and duty! This abuse of marriage is, in fact, an offense against nature, and is no doubt bitterly offensive to God. Though commonly spoken of, in a way of astonishing lightness, it is just that sin, by which every good possibility of the family is corrupted. What can two parents do for the child, they only submit to look upon, and take as a foundling to their care? If they have some degree of evidence in them that they are Christian disciples, they will have fatally clouded that evidence, by a contest with God's Providence, so irreverent to Him, and so cruel to their child. If now, at last, they somewhat love the child, which is theirs by compulsion, what office of a really Christian nurture can they fill in its behalf? They are under a complete and total disqualification, as respects the duties of their charge. They are out of rest in God, out of confidence toward Him, hindered in their prayers, lost to that sweetness of love and peace which ought to be the element of their house. Delving on thus, from such a point of beginning, and assuming the possible chance of success, in what they may do in the spirit of such a beginning, is simply absurd. What can they do in training a child for God, which they have accepted, at his hands, only as being thrust upon them by compulsion?

I might speak of other disqualifications that have a similar character, as implying some disagreement with Providence. But it must suffice to say generally, that there can be no such thing as a genuine Christian nurture that is out of peace with Cod's Providence--in any respect. On the contrary, it is when that peace is the element of the house, and sweetens every thing in it--pain, sickness, loss, the bitter cup of poverty, every ill of adversity or sting of wrong--then it is, and there, as nowhere else, that children are most sure to grow up into God's beauty, and a blessed and good life. The child that is born to such keeping, and lovingly lapped in the peaceful trust of Providence, is born to a glorious heritage. On the other hand, where the endeavor and life-struggle of the house, is, at bottom, a fight with Providence; envious, eager, anxious, out of content, out of rest, full of complaint and railings, it is impossible that any thing Christian should grow in such an element. The disqualification is complete.

Another whole class of disqualifications require to be named by themselves; those I mean which are caused by a bad or false morality in the parties, at some point where the failure is not suspected, and misses being corrected by the slender and very partial experience of their discipleship.

They are persons, for example, who make much of principles in their words, and really think that they are governed by principles, when, in fact, they do every thing for some reason of policy, and value their principles, more entirely than they know, for what they are worth in the computations of policy. Contrivance, artifice, or sometimes cunning, is the element of the house. A subtle, inveterate habit of scheming creeps into all the reasons of duty; and duty is done, not for duty's sake, but for the reasons, or prudential benefits to be secured by it. Even the praying of the house takes on a prudential air, much as if it were done for some reason not stated. A stranger in the house, seeing no scandalous wrong, but a fine show of principle, has a certain sense of coldness upon him, which he can not account for. How much of true Christian nurture there may be in such a house, it is not difficult to judge. Here, probably, is going to be one of the cases, where everybody wonders that children brought up so correctly, turn out so badly. It is not understood that such children were brought up to know principles, only as a stunted undergrowth of prudence, and that now the result appears.

Again there is, in some persons, who appear, in all other respects, to be Christian, a strange defect of truth or truthfulness. They are not conscious of it. They would take it as a cruel injustice, were they only to suspect their acquaintances of holding such an estimate of them. And yet there is a want of truth in every sort of demonstration they make. It is not their words only that lie, but their voice, air, action, their every putting forth has a lying character. The atmosphere they live in is an atmosphere of pretense. Their virtues are affectations. Their compassions and sympathies are the airs they put on. Their friendship is their mood and nothing more. And yet they do not know it. They mean, it may be, no fraud. They only cheat themselves so effectually as to believe, that what they are only acting is their truth. And, what is difficult to reconcile, they have a great many Christian sentiments, they maintain prayer as a habit, and will sometimes speak intelligently of matters of Christian experience. But how dreadful must be the effect of such a character, on the simple, trustful soul of a little child. When

the *crimen falsi* is in every thing heard, and looked upon, and done, he may grow up into a hypocrite, or a thief, but what shall make him a genuine Christian?

In the same manner, I could go on to show a multitude of disqualifications for the office of a genuine Christian nurture, that are created by a bad or defective morality, in parents who live a credibly Christian life. They make a great virtue, it may be, of frugality or economy, and settle every thing into a scale of insupportable parsimony and meanness. Or, they make a praise of generous living, and run it into a profligate and spendthrift habit. Or, they make such a virtue of honor and magnanimity, as to set the opinions and principles of men in deference, above the principles of God. Or, they get their chief motives of action out of the appearance of virtue, and not out of its realities. There is no end to the impostures of bad morality, that find a place in the lives of reputably Christian persons. They are generally too subtle to be detected by the inspection of their consciousness, and very commonly pass unobserved by others. And yet they have power to poison the nurture of the house, even though it appears to be, in some respects, Christian. Hence the profound necessity that Christian parents, consciously meaning to bring up their children for God, should make a thorough inspection of their morality itself, to find if there by any bad spot in it; knowing that, as certainly as there is, it will more or less fatally corrupt their children.

We have still another whole class of disqualifications to speak of, that belong, as vices, to the Christian life itself, and will, as much more certainly, be ruinous in their effects. Some of them would never be thought of as disqualifications for the Christian training of children, and yet they are so, in a degree to even cut off the reasonable hope of success. Probably a great part of the cases of disaster, that occur in the training of Christian families, are referable to these Christian vices, which are commonly not put down as evidences of apostasy, or any radical defect of Christian principle, because they are not supposed to imply a discontinuance of prayer, or a fatal subjection to the spirit of this world.

Sanctimony, for example, as we commonly use the term, is one of these vices. It describes what we conceive to be a saintly, or over-saintly air and manner, when there is a much inferious degree of sanctity in the life. There is no hypocrisy in it, for there is no intention to deceive; but there is a legal, austere, conscientiousness, which keeps on all the solemnities and longitudes of expression, just because there is too little of God's love and joy in the feeling, to play in the smiles of gladness and liberty. Now it is the little child's way, to get his first lessons from the looks and faces round him. And what can be worse, or do more to set him off from all piety, by a fixed aversion, than to have gotten such impressions of it only, as he takes from this always unblessed, tedious, look of sanctimony. What can a poor child do, when the sense of nature and natural life, the smiles, glad voices, and cheerful notes of play, are all overcast and gloomed, or, as it were, forbidden, by that ghostly piety in which it is itself being brought up? And yet the world will wonder immensely at the strange perversity of the child that grows up under such a saintly training, to be known as a person mortally averse to religion! Why, it would be a much greater wonder if he could think of it even with patience!

Bigotry is another of these Christian vices, and yet no one will assume his infallible capacity, in the matter of Christian training, as confidently as the bigot. Has he not the truth? Is he not opposite, as possible, to all error? has any man a greater abhorrence of all laxity and all variation from the standards? Is he not in a way of speaking out always, and giving faithful testimonies in his house? Yes, that must be admitted; and yet he is a man that mauls every truth of God, and every gentle and lovely feeling of a genuinely Christian character. His intensities are made by his narrowness and hate, and not by his love. He fills the house with a noise of piety, and may dog his children possibly into some kind of conformity with his opinions. But he is much more likely, by this brassy din, to only stun their intelligence and make them capable of any true religious impressions. There is no class of children that turn out worse, in general, than the children of the Christian bigots. . . .

* * * * * * * * *

The relationship between Darwin, Spencer, and Bushnell was not intentionally forged. Rather, their ideas mingled "stew-like" in the common sensical notions of progress, education, and the child present in the turn of the century American social reality.

Starting Points

John Dewey

Whereas it was Charles Darwin who most powerfully shaped the church's educational enterprise in an *indirect* and pervasive way, it was John Dewey who introduced Darwinism to the church's educational enterprise in a direct way by means of research and scholarship. By all standards, John Dewey was the most popular philosophical and educational influence in twentieth century American mainline religious education. Born on a farm in Burlington, Vermont the year Darwin published his *The Origin of Species* (1859), Dewey came to be identified with *pragmatism* (or what he called instrumentalism). In general terms, pragmatism concluded at least three things: 1) ideas that did not transform action were not worth consideration; 2) truth was viewed as an heuristic hypothesis resulting from careful and scientifically appropriate method, and 3) humans were the ground of all knowledge; transcendence in any traditional theological categories was discounted. The question, "Does it work?" unfairly stereotypes philosophical pragmatism. Yet, the inherent assumption that the determination of truth becomes a process of allowing the "fittest truths" to survive and the "weaker truths" to perish is essentially correct.

It is important to note that the leaders of public education and of religious education greatly influenced each other at the turn of the twentieth century. It is no surprise, then, that many of Dewey's educational and philosophical assumptions were adopted and adapted by leading scholars in the religious education movement. Three concepts that forcefully entered into critical conversation in regard to religious educational theory and practice at the turn of the century primarily by means of John Dewey were: democracy, ideal, and "steps" for reflection. While Dewey was not a theologian, his perspectives had great import for relating education and theology in religious education.

* * * * * * * * * *

John Dewey
(1916)

[From *Democracy and Education: An Introduction to the Philosophy of Education* (New York: The Macmillan Company, 1916), pp. 100-102.]

The Democratic Ideal.--The two elements in our criterion both point to democracy. The first signifies not only more numerous and more varied points of shared common interest, but greater reliance upon the recognition of mutual interests as a factor in social control. The second means not only freer interaction between social groups (once isolated so far as intention could keep up a separation) but change in social habit--its continuous readjustment through meeting the new situations produced by varied intercourse. And these two traits are precisely what characterize the democratically constituted society.

Upon the educational side, we note first that the realization of a form of social life in which interests are mutually interpenetrating, and where progress, or readjustment, is an important consideration, makes a democratic community more interested than other communities have cause to be in deliberate and systematic education. The devotion of democracy to education is a familiar fact. The superficial explanation is that a government resting upon popular suffrage cannot be successful unless those who elect and who obey their governors are educated. Since a democratic society repudiates the principle of external authority, it must find a substitute in voluntary disposition and interest; these can be created only by education. But there is a deeper explanation. A democracy is more than a form of government; it is primarily a mode of associated living, of conjoint communicated experience. The extension in space of the number of individuals who participate in an interest so that each has to refer his own action to that of others, and to consider the action of others to give point and direction to his own, is equivalent to the breaking down of those barriers of class, race, and national territory which kept men from perceiving the full import of their activity. These more numerous and more varied points of contact denote a greater diversity of stimuli to which an individual has to respond; they consequently put a premium on variation in his action. They secure a liberation of powers which remain suppressed as long as the incitations to action are partial, as they must be in a group which in its exclusiveness shuts out many interests.

The widening of the area of shared concerns, and the liberation of a greater diversity of personal capacities which characterize a democracy, are not of course the produce of deliberation and conscious effort. On the contrary, they were caused by the development of modes of manufacture and commerce, travel, migration, and intercommunication which flowed from the command of science over natural energy. But after greater individualization on one hand, and a broader community of interest on the other have come into existence, it is a matter of deliberate effort to sustain and extend them. Obviously a society to which stratification into separate classes would be fatal, must see to it that intellectual opportunities are accessible to all on equable and easy terms. A society marked off into classes need to be specially attentive only to the education of its ruling elements. A society which is mobile, which is full of channels for the distribution of a change occurring anywhere, must see to it that its members are educated to personal initiative and adaptability. Otherwise, they will be overwhelmed by the changes in which they are caught and whose significance or connections they do not perceive. The result will be a confusion in which a few will appropriate to themselves the results of the blind and externally directed activities of others.

* * * * * * * * * *

John Dewey

(1934)

[From *A Common Faith* (New Haven: Yale University Press, 1934), pp. 18-19, 43, 50-51, 84.]

The connection between imagination and the harmonizing of the self is closer than is usually thought. The idea of a whole, whether of the whole personal being or of the world, is an imaginative, not a literal, idea. The limited world of our observation and reflection becomes the Universe only through imaginative extension. It cannot be apprehended in knowledge nor realized in reflection. Neither observation, thought, nor practical activity can attain that complete unification of the self which is called a whole. The *whole* self is an ideal, an imaginative projection. Hence the idea of a thoroughgoing and deep-seated harmonizing of the self with the Universe (as a name for the totality of conditions with which the self is connected) operates only through imagination--which is one reason why this composing of the self is not voluntary in the sense of an act of special volition or resolution. An "adjustment" possesses the will rather than is its express product. Religionists have been right in thinking of it as an influx from sources beyond conscious deliberation and purpose --a fact that helps explain, psychologically, why it has so generally been attributed to a supernatural source and that, perhaps, throws some light upon the reference of it by William James to unconscious factors. And it is pertinent to note that the unification of the self throughout the ceaseless flux of what it does, suffers, and achieves, cannot be attained in terms of itself. The self is always directed toward something beyond itself and so its own unification depends upon the idea of the integration of the shifting scenes of the world into that imaginative totality we call the Universe. . . .

The idea that "God" represents a unification of ideal values that is essentially imaginative in origin when the imagination supervenes in conduct is attended with verbal difficulties

owing to our frequent use of the word "imagination" to
denote fantasy and doubtful reality. But the reality of ideal
ends as ideals is vouched for by their undeniable power in
action. An ideal is not an illusion because imagination is the
organ through which it is apprehended. For *all* possibilities
reach us through the imagination. In a definite sense the only
meaning that can be assigned the term "imagination" is that
things unrealized in fact come home to us and have power to
stir us. The unification effected through imagination is not
fanciful, for it is the reflex of the unification of practical and
emotional attitudes. The unity signifies not a single Being,
but the unity of loyalty and effort evoked by the fact that
many ends are one in the power of their ideal, or imaginative,
quality to stir and hold us. . . .

These considerations may be applied to the idea of God, or,
to avoid misleading conceptions, to the idea of the divine.
This idea is, as I have said, one of ideal possibilities unified
through imaginative realization and projection. But this idea
of God, or of the divine, is also connected with all the natural
forces and conditions--including man and human association-
-that promote the growth of the ideal and that further its
realization. We are in the presence neither of ideals
completely embodied in existence nor yet of ideals that are
mere rootless ideals, fantasies, utopias. For there are forces
in nature and society that generate and support the ideals.
They are further unified by the action that gives them
coherence and solidity. It is this *active* relation between ideal
and actual to which I would give the name "God." I would
not insist that the name *must* be given. There are those who
hold that the associations of the term with the supernatural
are so numerous and close that any use of the word "God" is
sure to give rise to misconception and be taken as a
concession to traditional ideas.

They may be correct in this view. But the facts to which I
have referred are there, and they need to be brought out with
all possible clearness and force. There exist concretely and
experimentally goods--the values of art in all its forms, of
knowledge, of effort and of rest after striving, of education
and fellowship, of friendship and love, of growth in mind and

body. These goods are there and yet they are relatively embryonic. Many persons are shut out from generous participation in them; there are forces at work that threaten and sap existent goods as well as prevent their expansion. A clear and intense conception of a union of ideal ends with actual conditions is capable of arousing steady emotion. It may be fed by every experience, no matter what its material. .
. .

Lip service--often more than lip service--has been given to the idea of the common brotherhood of all men. But those outside the fold of the church and those who do not rely upon belief in the supernatural have been regarded as only potential brothers, still requiring adoption into the family. I cannot understand how any realization of the democratic ideal as a vital moral and spiritual ideal in human affairs is possible without surrender of the conception of the basic division to which supernatural Christianity is committed. Whether or no we are, save in some metaphorical sense, all brothers, we are at least a%l in the same boat traversing the same turbulent ocean. The potential religious significance of this fact is infinite.

* * * * * * * * *

John Dewey
(1910)

[From *How We Think* (Boston: D.C. Heath & Co., 1910), pp. 68-78.]

PART TWO: LOGICAL CONSIDERATIONS

THE ANALYSIS OF A COMPLETE ACT OF THOUGHT

In this chapter we shall make an analysis of the process of thinking into its steps or elementary constituents, basing the analysis upon descriptions of a number of extremely simple, but genuine, cases of reflective experience. . . .

Upon examination, each instance reveals, more or less clearly, five logically distinct steps: (i) a felt difficulty; (ii) its location and definition; (iii) suggestion of possible solution; (iv) development by reasoning of the bearings of the suggestion; (v) further observation and experiment leading to its acceptance or rejection; that is, the conclusion of belief or disbelief.

1. The first and second steps frequently fuse into one. The difficulty may be felt with sufficient definiteness as to set the mind at once speculating upon its probable solution, or an undefined uneasiness and shock may come first, leading only later to definite attempt to find out what is the matter. Whether the two steps are distinct or blended, there is the factor emphasized in our original account of reflection--v~z. the perplexity or problem... The problem *if the discovery of intervening terms which when inserted between the remoter end and the given means will harmonize them with each other....*

2. As already noted, the first two steps, the feeling of a discrepance, or difficulty, and the acts of observation that serve to define the character of the difficulty may, in a given instance, telescope together. In cases of striking novelty or unusual perplexity, the difficulty, however, is likely to present itself at first as a shock, as emotional disturbance, as a more or less vague feeling of the unexpected, of something queer, strange, funny, or disconcerting. In such instances, there are

necessary observations deliberately calculated to bring to light just what is the trouble, or to make clear the specific character of the problem. In large measure, the existence or nonexistence of this step makes the difference between reflection proper, or safeguarded *critical* inference and uncontrolled thinking. Where sufficient pains to locate the difficulty are not taken, suggestions for its resolution must be more or less random. . . .

3. The third factor is suggestion. The situation in which the perplexity occurs calls up something not present to the senses... (a) Suggestion is the very heart of inference; it involves going from what is present to something absent. Hence, it is more or less speculative, adventurous. Since inference goes beyond what is actually present, it involves a leap, a jump, the propriety of which cannot be absolutely warranted in advance, no matter what precautions be taken. Its control is indirect, on the one hand, involving the formation of habits of mind which are at once enterprising and cautious; and on the other hand, involving the selection and arrangement of the particular facts upon perception of which suggestion issues. (b) The suggested conclusion so far as it is not accepted but only tentatively entertained constitutes an idea. Synonyms for this are *supposition, conjecture, guess, hypothesis,* and (in elaborate cases *theory*). Since suspended belief, or the postponement of a final conclusion pending further evidence, depends partly upon the presence of rival conjectures as to the best course to pursue or the probable explanation to favor, *cultivation of a variety of alternative suggestions* is an important factor in good thinking.

4. The process of developing the bearings--or, as they are more technically termed, the *implications*--of any idea with respect to any problem, is termed *reasoning*. . . .

Reasoning has the same effect upon a suggested solution as more intimate and extensive observation has upon the original problem. Acceptance of the suggestion in its first form is prevented by looking into it more thoroughly. Conjectures that seem plausible at first sight are often found

unfit or even absurd when their full consequences are traced
out. Even when reasoning out the bearings of a supposition
does not lead to rejection, it develops the idea into a form in
which it is more apposite to the problem. . . .

5. The concluding and conclusive step is some kind of
experimental   corroboration,   or   verification,   of   the
conjectural idea.   Reasoning shows that *if* the idea be
adopted, certain consequences follow. So far the conclusion
is hypothetical or conditional. If we look and find present all
the conditions demanded by the theory, and if we find the
characteristic traits called for by rival alternatives to be
lacking, the tendency to believe, to accept, is almost
irresistible.   Sometimes   direct   observation   furnished
corroboration, as in the case of the pole on the boat. In other
cases, as in that of the bubbles, experiment is required; that
is, *conditions are deliberately arranged in accord with the
requirements of an idea or hypothesis to see if the results
theoretically indicated by the idea actually occur.* . . .

Observation exists at the beginning and again at the end of
the process: at the beginning, to determine more definitely
and precisely the nature of the difficulty to be dealt with; at
the end, to test the value of some hypothetically entertained
conclusion. Between those two termini of observation, we
find the more distinctively *mental* aspects of the entire
thought-cycles: (i) inference, the suggestion of an
explanation or solution; and (ii) reasoning, the development
of the bearings and implications of the suggestion. . . .

The disciplined, or logically trained, mind--the aim of the
educative process--is the mind able to judge how far each of
these steps needs to be carried in any particular situation. No
cast-iron rules can be laid down. Each case has to be dealt
with as it arises, on the basis of its importance and of the
context in which it occurs. To take too much pains in one
case is as foolish--as illogical--as to take too little in another.
At one extreme, almost any conclusion that insures prompt
and unified action may be better than any long delayed
conclusion; while at the other, decision may have to be
postponed for a long period--perhaps for a life-time. The
trained mind is the one that best grasps the degree of

observation, forming of ideas, reasoning, and experimental testing required in any special case, and that profits the most, in future thinking, by mistakes made in the past. What is important is that the mind should be sensitive to problems and skilled in methods of attack and solution.

* * * * * * * * *

It would not be reductionistic to conclude that for the first half of the twentieth century, American mainline religious educators were attempting to integrate the findings of Darwin and Spencer (mediated through the pragmatic philosophical perspective of Dewey) and of Bushnell. The result was a creative tension between theological and educational concerns.

The Rise of the Liberal Era

Coe, Bower, Chave, Fahs, Elliott

Informed by the new educational philosophy of John Dewey, and inspired by the implications of Bushnell's understanding of nurture ("that the child is to grow up a Christian, and never know himself as being otherwise"), the progressive-liberal movement in religious education dominated the arena of American Protestant mainline educational thought for about the first fifty years of the twentieth century. It must be noted that some of the most careful and critical thinking about religious education emerged from the progressive-liberal movement. Crucial figures in this movement were George Albert Coe, William Clayton Bower, Ernest Chave, Sophia L. Fahs, and Harrison S. Elliott. The following selections from these leaders of progressive-liberal religious education give the immediate impression of educational vigor and scholarly competence. They also give the impression of a characteristically American optimism in democracy, science, and progress. George Albert Coe is, beyond all doubt, dean of the twentieth century American Protestant progressive-liberal educational movement. Professor at Union Theological Seminary, New York, and one of the founders of the Religious Education Association, Coe was known for his vigorous scholarship and humble friendliness. William Clayton Bower, professor of religious education at the College of the Bible in Lexington, Kentucky, was the leading progressive-liberal mind in curriculum theory for religious education. Ernest Chave, a Canadian Baptist minister who studied under John Dewey, was a leading figure in the International Council of Religious Education. He also served as

Professor of Religious Education in the Divinity School of the
University of Chicago. His strong views on faith and God are very
reminiscent of Dewey's found in *A Common Faith*. Sophia L. Fahs, an
Unitarian minister, taught at Union Theological Seminary, New York,
and is perhaps best known as the editor of curriculum materials for
religious education in the American Unitarian Association. Harrison S.
Elliott was professor of Practical Theology and Director of the
Department of Religious Education and Psychology at Union
Theological Seminary, New York, for twenty-seven years (replacing
George Albert Coe). His *Can Religious Education Be Christian?* was
the last major attempt to defend/define the progressive-liberal
perspective. It is not incorrect to suggest that his book signaled the end
of a once vigorous and vital movement in American religious education.

                    * * * * * * * * * *

                                    George Albert Coe
                                       (1929)

[From *What is Christian Education?* (New York: Charles Scribner's
Sons, 1929), pp. 40-59, 296.]

              Transmissive Education Hands On Our Faults,
                But Conceals Them, and by Concealment
                       Adds To Their Prestige

     "Transmissive education" is here adopted as a short name
for policies and practices that are based upon the assumption
that the primary purpose of education, by which its particular
processes are to be controlled and judged, is the perpetuation
of an already existing culture or some part of it. "Creative
education," on the other hand, will be our term for education
that places in this position of primacy a purpose to improve
or reconstruct a culture or some part of it, and that employs
transmission processes--always present anyhow--to this end.
     Transmissive education intends... to hand on what is good
in our present culture without perpetuating its defects.
Hence it selects for teaching purposes the finer specimens of

humanity and its products, representing them as the true reality. Thus: We are neighbors, the true neighbor does so and so, and here are examples of true neighborliness; we are America, the true America does so and so, as these instances show; here is the church, and the church is such and such a fellowship; and here is Christianity, which means thus and so. In each case, that which we approve in a thing is represented as the essence of it. In none of this is there any intention to misrepresent actualities, of course, but only to give force to ideals.

This means, however, selected silences as well as selected material of text-book and of teacher-talk--selected silences that are supposed to block off the channels through which our defects, if we mentioned them, might transmit themselves. But see how this combination of sound and silence works. The school, the text-book, the pulpit does not really block the road between our faults and the mind of the learner. He knows us in a thousand ways that our intended education of him does not control. We may tell him that Christians do not set their hearts upon worldly possessions, but even a child knows that Christians do exactly this. We may illustrate the Christian spirit by picturing a hero, a saint, or Jesus, but the learner, through his myriad contacts with us, naturally assumes that the picture represents something exceptional, remote, not Christianity as a present, going, practical concern.

This mixture, in the learner's mind, of what we offer him as our teaching and what our conduct displays under no such name as "material of instruction" has the following effect: Two mental categories are formed, in one of which he places, with a sentimental approval that is not insincere, the ideal formula or picture, but in the other of which he bestows his understanding of how life actually is lived here and now, together with some sense of participation in it upon its own terms.

He assents, that is to say, to both his teacher, the one who is called teacher, and the other who is not. Which of these teachers and teachings will ordinarily be the more influential

with him is scarcely a problem. Moreover, what often looks
like a big, dark mystery--the enormous moral inefficiencies of
the well-meaning--now begins to clear up. The well-meaning
live in two world, both of which they take at face value, a
world of sentiment and a world of practicality. They can live
in these two worlds without hypocrisy because they have
been receptive, not critical, toward both teachers.
Transmissive education is the secret.

That our efforts to teach religion are largely counteracted
by the learner's contacts with the life of our time has been
lamented by many, but no likely remedy is proposed. The
reason why we cannot think of a remedy is that we only half
perceive the nature of the problem. There is also another
fact, not yet mentioned, that is determinative, namely, that
our Christian teaching itself transmits our faults and gives
them prestige.

The mind of the learner cannot be divided into completely
water-tight compartments. Personality is unitary; it
spontaneously seeks, more or less blindly, to be consistent
with itself. Can we at all trace, then, this consistency-
creating process in the mind of the learner whom we have
described? We can, to some extent. Let us begin with the
use of terms--"Christian" for example. This adjective is
applied to both the "ideal essence" of our religion and the
unideal men whom we meet, their unideal piety, and the
unideal church which they compose and manage. Some
assimilation of one of these meanings to the other is bound to
take place unless somehow the contrariety of them is rubbed
into the mind. But a rubbing-in policy is lacking. Our silence
concerning the defects of Christianity permits the learner's
mind, even when it touched the most vital things of our faith,
to be unwatchful, desultory, and yet receptive. Under these
conditions, the meaning of "Christian is of course assimilated
to the concrete actualities, here and now before the mind,
that bear this name. By this process, though you teach ideals
without end, the learner will slump from his ideal sentiments
into conformity with things as they are.

What is more, the social prestige of the church, its accepted
authority as teacher, and the sentiment of the ideal that is

fostered by it, all participate in this process of self-unification. Thus it is that Christian education, by silences imposed by the transmission theory, in effect sanctions, if it does not actually sanctify, our common and tolerated faults. It is, unintentionally, a way of maintaining the existing low level of religious respectability.

The extent and the force of this silence are little less than amazing. Every religious communion, local or denominational, is a scene of contradictions and conflicts within the moral and spiritual realm. There are uncertainties as to what is right and best, and opinions differ; what thinks itself to be idealism locks horns with what regards itself as practicality; agitated conscience thrusts at yesterday's goodness, and prudence and courage debate with each other. Mistakes are made, many of them. But all this living, breathing actuality, so well adapted to awaken thought and illuminate the judgment, is outside the curriculum. The learner gets no training in the analysis of such situations; as a rule he does not know what happens "on the inside," does not know what blunders are made, and is not put on guard against repeating them, and, conversely, he does not understand or appreciate creative acts when they occur. Every old and obstinate defect in our ecclesiastical life perpetuates itself generation after generation through pupils who are taught to be loyal without being taught to discriminate. Transmissive education is particularly adept in handing on our sins of omission--and in building tombs for prophets!

Transmissive Education Employs Either Force
or Evasion in the Interest of Effectiveness

As long as men believed that coercing the body could control the mind, the self-constituted wielders of educational authority, whether in state or in church, used physical force as a means for propagating a culture or a faith. They were logical in doing so. For if we grant the transmissive conception of education, the coercion is good if it really does hammer in the idea, the standard, or the habit that we desire to hand on.

When it was perceived that physical force does not accomplish what was expected of it, resort was had to psychical compulsion or strong pressure. It took three forms: Compulsion by supposedly logical demonstration, habituation through repetition, and restraint through fear. The first, or intellectual compulsion, affected chiefly older pupils, as in colleges and theological seminaries. It was somewhat generally practised by Protestants two generations ago in the teaching of what was called "Christian evidences"; it is a stated practice of Catholics, and apparently it must remain so as long as the basic position of the church is dogmatic and intellectualistic. The second form of psychic compulsion or pressure--habituation by repetition--is represented by the memorization of catechisms; the third form, fear, by warnings against the sinfulness of unbelief, and by sundry well-remembered representations of God and the future life.

Protestant religious education has moved away from the use of both physical and psychical compulsion, but it has unwittingly fallen into the use of evasions. Thus:

(a) Appeals are made to the learner's intelligence, by invitations to examine evidence, just as if really free judgment were intended, but if he does not reach the preconceived conclusions of his teacher or of the church, if he balks at accepting what they seek to transmit to him, there follows social displeasure and sometimes a kind of religious outlawing.

(b) Attempts are made to induce a favorable judgment upon the Bible, biblical characters, and the church, by stating excellences without mentioning limitations and defects.

(c) The Scriptures are commonly used in worship as if all the parts employed were upon the same level of historic fact or spiritual illumination, with the result of confusing actual events with imagined ones, giving the color of finality to the views and peculiarities of biblical writers, and even mixing Christian and sub-Christian motives and standards.

(d) What may be called emotional subreption is resorted to, that is, causing the pupil to believe that a doctrine that has been historically associated with an experience that is valuable to him is essentially one with the experience.

(e) There is habitual use, especially in worship, of the phrases and the formulae of obsolete or obsolescent beliefs or attitudes, with no warning that this is the fact.

(f) Our faith is stated in the presence of the laity or of the young in terms so general as to conceal issues known by theologians to be there. By the use of euphuistic generalities we may avoid controversy, but we also become character less.

(g) Suggestion is used in such a way as to promote an institutional loyalty that is narrower than we should be willing openly to defend. Much talk about *our* church, coupled with silence about other bodies of Christians, has remarkable power to keep the horizon from enlarging.

These evasions do not occur equally everywhere, but all of them are common and most of them are almost universal in Protestantism. The explanation is not that we are human, fallible, and careless. These evasions flow directly from the assumed necessity of making the transmission-idea work under modern conditions. The truth is, of course, that it doesn't really work; these items are direct evidence of departure from the theory. And the profitableness of this departure is worse than doubtful. It does make adherence to a church easier; it may produce lip-loyalty to ancient creeds, and it may prolong old usages; but it produces also quiet doubt, dissent, disinterest, and unobtrusive absence. There is increasing comment to the effect that the note of reality does not ring clearly.

Transmissive Education, Its Eyes Fixed Upon Content, Is Slow to Apprehend the Forces at Work

If I assume that I have exactly what you need, I lack a motive for watching your symptoms. Transmissive education, confident that it has in its keeping the solution of all spiritual problems, does not feel that rigorous analysis of changing conditions is of prime importance to it.   The teacher's attention is naturally upon something that is to be brought out of the past into the present, not upon the forces at work in the immediate environment.   Here is a material part of the explanation of three deep-seated defects in the teaching work of the church. They are frequently recognized and deplored; but what keeps them so alive and respectable?

(a) There is something like general recognition of the fact that Protestantism as a whole, in this country at least, is attempting to transmit Christianity through teachers who, as a rule, are incompetent as teachers but competent as Christians. Granted the transmission theory, this is not as illogical as it seems to be.   For, when religion is to be delivered in original packages, anybody may be the carrier of it who is loyal to the task. We shall not fully understand the almost universal lack of trained teachers until we perceive that their task has been to hand on something in which they take no creative or responsible part.   Assuming that a "message" is what does the essential religious work, we fail to appreciate the dynamics of the human beings immediately in our presence.

Thus it is that Christian missions, until experience brings disillusionment, assume that their essential business is to "declare" the Gospel. Upon this notion was based the former rallying-cry of the Student Volunteers, "The evangelization of the world in this generation." The central act of Christian education, accordingly, was taken to be the presentation of a given ideational content, as the bible or Christian doctrines. A formal, question-and-answer catechism actually has been taught to African natives, so a missionary to "the dark continent tells me.   This is exceptional, no doubt; nevertheless it is illuminating. It is an extreme case of the same state of mind that assumed that any missionary is competent to teach a Bible class. And indeed, since any missionary is a Christian, it follows--if the "message" is what makes one a Christian--that every missionary carries in himself the instrument for doing the work; all he has to do is to set this instrument going.

This is one root-cause of poor teaching at home as well as in mission fields. It is a habit with us, when we contemplate our untrained teaching force, to say to ourselves, "But these teachers are devoted Christians, and somehow Christianity will flow through them into their pupils." The partial truth that this contains makes the error in it all the more specious. Something of the ideal called Christianity will flow through the teacher, but much else will flow through him at the same time. His method as teacher may even obstruct or conceal what he wants to teach. This is a mere commonplace, of course; nevertheless it never will be duly heeded until education becomes a fresh approach to the dynamics of living rather than the handing-on of a content or a prescription. The solution of the problem of teacher-training awaits the determination of this prior question.

(b) The transmission theory leads directly to a misconception of the nature of technic in teaching. Technic is assumed to be merely instrumental and external to the thin curriculum-makers and the text-book writers.

The subjection of the laity to the hierarchy in Catholicism is open and above board. The government is an absolute monarchy; it does not pretend to be anything else. There are, however, powers behind the throne. There are reasons why this man rather than another is elected to the papal chair; there are reasons why the Pope chooses this or that man for bishop; promotion within the hierarchy depends upon conditions not stated; the Pope listens to advice, and influences of many sorts play upon him as upon you and me. He does not claim to be infallible in all that he does, in fact; but, since the faithful have no way of dividing between the obligation of absolute obedience and the obligation of respect for the Holy Father, they obey whatever is transmitted through the hierarchy. Thus, even in Catholicism, which is so daringly logical, we have a supposed obedience to God that includes subjection to men in matters in which they do not even claim to be infallible.

The transmission theory of education has no view of authority to offer that will not involve this or some parallel confusion between the commandments of men and the ordinances of God. If we ascribe authority to revelation, we submit to theologians; if we ascribe authority to church, we submit, not to the ideal church, which "never was on land or sea," but to any men who happen to have won control; if we make "Christian experience" our authority, we submit to those who have defined and delimited the terms "Christian" and "experience."

The Best Contribution of Transmissive Education Is Its Byproducts. It is Weakest Where It Thinks It Is Strongest

Ask a thousand men what was the most powerful influence for good that Christian education brought into their lives, and many more than nine hundred will make replies like the following: It was the teacher's own character; it was the genuineness of a parent's religion, or a love that would not let me go; it was a personal touch at a crisis-point in my life; it was a fellowship that kept me straight until good habits were firmly established. Granted that this is not a precise or scientific test, and that our untested judgments concerning the dynamics of our own personality are subject to a very wide margin of error. Nevertheless, the general, almost unanimous swing of men's judgments in this matter is impressive, and it is in line with the most rigidly scientific knowledge of character-dynamics that we have.[1] We are safe in saying that the mainly effective factor in Christian education is 'the Word made flesh'--that is, the human relations that accompany the teaching rather than the content of the teaching.

But these excellent by-products are partly or wholly offset, as we have seen, by a dilution-process that is inherent in transmissive education. It lays its chief stress upon handing down something out of the past, yet of its own nature, as our analysis has shown, it devitalizes this very thing. The great, the overwhelmingly great, defect at this point is failure to employ the enormous potentiality that actually does reside in the message. Let us, then, close this review of why we fail by contemplating the height and the depth of meaning in such ancient words as these:

> Love your neighbor as yourself.
>
> Love your enemies.
>
> God is love.
>
> He that hath done it unto the least of these hath done it unto me.
>
> He that seeks to save his life shall lose it.
>
> He that is greatest among you shall be the servant of all.
>
> Seek first the rule and righteousness of God.
>
> What shall it profit a man if he shall gain the whole world and lose his own life?
>
> It is easier for a camel to pass through the eye of a needle than for a rich man to enter the Kingdom.
>
> Not every one that saith unto me, "Lord, Lord," but he that doeth the will of my Father.
>
> Thou shalt love the Lord, thy God, with all thy heart.

No one, I think, will challenge the following opinion: Most Americans who have received Christian instruction perceive no inconsistency between the principles here enunciated and the philosophy of "preparedness" for war; no inconsistency with our selfish and self-willed nationalism; no inconsistency with our national superiority-complex, nor with our current superiority-complexes with regard to races, classes, and religions; no inconsistency with sex-inequality in the family, the church, and society generally; no inconsistency with an economic system that values profits above personality.

Recently a most eminent American preacher asked a great ecclesiastical assembly this question: "Isn't it time to take Jesus seriously?" When critics asked why it was that the World War could occur in the western world, which already had had the gospel of peace before it for centuries, defenders of the faith were quick to reply, "Christianity never has been tried." Never has been tried! That is, the church of each generation, when it supposed it was transmitting the revelation of God that is in Jesus, actually transmitted its own half-blind and faulty ways.

CODA

What, Then, Is Christian Education?

It is the systematic, critical examination and reconstruction of relations between persons, guided by Jesus' assumption that persons are of infinite worth, and by the hypothesis of the existence of God, the Great Valuer of Persons.

* * * * * * * * * *

William Clayton Bower

[From *The Curriculum of Religious Education* (New York: Charles Scribners' Sons, 1925), pp. 95-101.]

At this point there emerges the second concept in this discussion. What is to be understood by the concept of control?

Control may mean, on the one hand, the compulsion, by the use of forces external to the person controlled, of one person or group of persons by another. It may assume the form of the coercion of one individual by another, of the individual by the institution or the social group, or of the masses by a powerful leader or minority. It assumes, in most instances, the control of the individual by the social group. In any case, the one who is under control is passive and obedient, while the one controlling is active and domineering. Always it consists of the imposition of the will and purposes of one upon another.

The instruments for the securing of external control have been many and varied. In its crudest aspect control has assumed the form of physical force. It is in this way that the state enforces its sovereignty upon its unwilling members by force to the uttermost, ultimately through military power. Another direct method of control has been through laws and regulations. These external devices have, in the last resort, depended upon an appeal to force to secure obedience to them, though advanced peoples acquire a legal attitude which renders an appeal to force less frequent. Physical force, however, is by no means the most effective instrument of external social control. Beyond certain limits force becomes self-limiting. Even more powerful instruments of control may be found among psychological influences. Among these are the various forms of social pressure of a non-preinstituted character which are made effective through various forms of approval or disapproval. One of the most effective forms of social control is prejudice, created by the withholding of facts, or the casting of the mind's action into the grooves of class, racial, partisan, or religious presuppositions. These prejudices form a kind of smooth rim around the mind from which thought rebounds inwardly upon itself. As a result, persons, without suspecting it, are slavishly bound to their group and to its ways of looking at things. No less effective is the obedience and conformity secured by the forming of rigid and unintelligent habits by the mature members of the group in the young during the period of their helpless immaturity, when they have neither the capacity nor the experience necessary to make an intelligent choice of the permanent habits that are to-dominate their later development, thus preventing a free and continuous personal growth. Not infrequently has education itself been used to coerce the minds of the young through selected information, mental bias, or fixed prejudices. Because of its very effectiveness in determining the minds of the young, education lends itself in an unusual manner to purposes of propaganda in the hands of powerful and interested leaders. Among all the instruments of external control none has historically proven more effective, and at the same time more destructive, than fear.

At the opposite extreme from external control is guidance.
Guidance works from within. In it the initiative is shared by
both the teacher and the learner. Both are active. Guidance
is secured through understanding, through the sharing of
experiences and purposes, and through friendly counsel. The
objective of guidance is not to weight, least of all to
overbear, the judgment and will of the learner. The function
of mature guidance is to help the immature to understand the
situation in which he finds himself, to break it up into its
constituent factors without overlooking important elements,
to help him feel and understand the problems involved, to
stimulate the suggestion of possible outcomes, to assist him
in discovering relevant sources of information, to assist him
in arriving at a choice after he has thought its consequences
through, and to encourage him to overcome obstacles and to
persist until he has seen his decision through. In it there is a
meeting of minds and purposes. In it there is the desire on
the part of the learner to understand sympathetically and
appreciatively the inherited points of view and processes of
the mature members of society, and an equal desire on the
part of the mature members of the group that these inherited
points of view and processes should be freshly criticised and
modified to meet the requirements of the oncoming
generation. In this way racial experience is steadied and given
continuity and at the same time room is made for continuous
reconstruction and improvement.

It thus appears that the concept of self-realization through
the enrichment of experience and the concept of social
control are not irreconcilable. They are mediated in and
through guidance that passes on to the learner the ideals,
possessions, and purposes of the group, that socializes him,
and that at the same time assists him in securing a firmness
and certainty in his control over his own experience. The
continuity of the interests of society is guaranteed by the
presence within society of individuals who have attained the
highest degree of self-realization, but who are, at the same
time, thoroughly socialized in their attitudes and motives. On
the other hand, as was pointed out in the discussion
concerning the nature of personality, it is impossible to

achieve a sense of self-hood, much less to arrive at the highest degree of self-realization, except within a free social medium in which persons are reacting upon persons.

We must, consequently, add to our two initial sources for the enrichment of experience, namely, meaning and worth, a third--the control of experience in the form of guidance. From the viewpoint of a self-realizing person as well as of the social group, an experience that is not under control is capricious, unreliable, dangerous, unsatisfying. Leading nowhere in particular, it is impossible that such an experience should further the person toward the realization of his purposes. An experience not under control is even much more likely to defeat his purposes than to further them.

Great as is the necessity of evaluating experiences from any point of view, it is especially urgent from the viewpoint of the educator. He may well give a minimum of attention to those types of experience that are slender in their educational resourcefulness and select those types that, because they are rich in possibilities, lend themselves to enrichment and the higher forms of co-operative control. Especially will he seize upon those multiple situations that are capable of evoking multiple responses because, in addition to carrying a proportionately large freightage of values, they provide the conditions that are necessary for reflective thinking, require that choices be made, and call for the exercise of a sustained and disciplined will.

We are prepared, from what has been said, to understand why it is that, given these experiences with large possibilities, the factors that lead to the enrichment of experience are also the same factors that lead to its intelligent and purposive direction.

The basic factor in the enrichment and control of experience is discrimination. As has already been suggested, the higher orders of experience arise from responses to multiple situations. And yet, no matter how varied and rich in stimuli a given situation may be, the effectiveness of the response will depend upon the mental approach of the person responding. The uncritical mind is likely to fall into one of three errors. It may see the situation as a confused mass without distinguishing among its separate elements, with the result that the response is a generalized and confused response, as though the situation were simple. Or it may fail to distinguish between the relevant and irrelevant elements in the situation, in which case the response may be entirely beside the mark and futile. Or still further, it may seize upon the wrong element, with the result that the response gives a totally wrong outcome and leads the person astray. Thus, in translating a foreign language it is necessary that the learner break up the situation into its essential elements. If this is not done, the learner merely guesses at the meaning of the confused sentence. If he fails to distinguish the essential forms of verb and noun endings that indicate mood and tense and person and case, his translation will be inaccurate and misleading. Precisely the same discrimination is required for accuracy in determining practical courses of action or in arriving at sound moral judgments. If the situation has been mentally fumbled through failure to break it up and seize upon the essential factor, the outcome in experience will not correspond to reality. The critical mind analyzes the situation by breaking it up into its constituent elements. It carefully scrutinizes each factor in order to judge whether it is relevant or irrelevant and whether the relevant factor will lead to a right or a wrong outcome as judged by the end to be attained. Having reached a clear judgment on this point, the critical mind seizes upon the essential factor and proceeds immediately to seeing the issue through. This is precisely the difference between the fuzzy-minded thinker and the person with a clear and dependable judgment. It is also, more than we have been wont to think, a fundamental quality of moral action.   The moral quality of actions goes back to this beginning point in conduct. It is not enough that one's intentions be good. It is morally incumbent upon normal persons that they think morally by thinking clearly and accurately. The foundations for all effective action as well as for moral action are laid in a mental attitude of critical analysis of situations and an accurate discrimination as to the relevancy of the factors involved. This is also the sound and necessary basis for precise scientific thinking, for all aesthetic judgment and appreciation, for the discernment and fulfillment of all social relations, and for an effective religious experience.

* * * * * * * * *

Ernest Chave

[From *A Functional Approach to Religious Education* (Chicago: The University of Chicago Press, 1947), pp. 92-98.]

QUEST FOR TRUTH AND REALIZATION OF VALUES

A healthy, growing child asks questions as soon as he can talk, and the more he learns the more he is likely to keep on asking questions. The normal reaction is for this spirit of inquiry to continue with increasing sense of the complexity but solvability of most problems, unless parents, teachers, or others repress and discourage this search for knowledge. School offers children opportunities to explore both present objects and processes and the learnings of the centuries. They discover change, growth, laws, and interesting possibilities of development, all of which give meaning and motivation toward fuller living. They learn to analyze problems and social issues into their component factors, to weigh their relative significance, and to formulate conclusions as to causes and effects. They learn to think with others, to exchange ideas, to understand reasons for different opinions, to use their own judgments, and to test the consequences of different plans. While modern education tends to put its emphasis upon learning to think critically and creatively, it recognizes the need for a body of knowledge. One cannot think without ideas, and it is foolish to discount the findings of men through the ages. Appreciation for the learnings of the past is, however, dependent upon each individual's own rich experience and active imagination. The learning of others cannot be transmitted without the mental and emotional response of interested persons. The educational method must therefore start from where an individual is and bring in experience of the race when interest in what others have thought and done is awakened. Sometimes education seems to give so much attention to the importance of each generation becoming familiar with the best ideas, attitudes, and methods of the past that it seems to ignore the psychological preparation necessary to make this meaningful and interesting. Learning does not begin with the past but with the present which the past has given us.

One illustration of the difficulty of using historical data and the need for critical creative thought when dealing with past records is shown in a sixth-grade unit on the history of Chicago. The children of a Chicago school were stimulated to see the possible value and fun in writing up the story of their city. The teacher made some records available; visits were made to several institutions where exhibits of historical materials were on display; newspapers and other records were examined; and a number of people were interviewed. The children found that they could get a fairly good outline of the history from the days of Indian settlements down to the present but that there were many details about which there were confusing and conflicting records. They tried to explain some of these contradictory accounts, and by comparing ideas and impressions they worked out together a fairly satisfactory story. The experience in this project was found useful in many later situations as they tried to reconstruct historical happenings and to interpret different points of view. It is the kind of mental discipline on specific, concrete material needed for examination of historical religious records and for constant differentiation between facts and interpretation of facts.

The religious educator turns repeatedly to the general educator who has the pupils five day a week to see what he is doing and what young people are learning. He finds him beset by different theorists, the classicists who emphasize historical content, the functionalists and experimentalists who want studies centered in the present world of experience, and the vocationalists who think of the practical tasks of making a living. All of these points of view have important elements for a well-educated person, and they should be organized into a balanced program. The two most pressing concerns are whether growing persons are being taught to think critically and creatively and whether they have an interest in using their own experience and skills, as well as general human experience, in the solution of personal-social problems. While it is valuable in a democracy for everyone to have a common body of ideas, values, and general attitudes, it is also desirable that a wide range of specialized knowledge and skills be developed.   Each individual should find opportunities in several areas of life for cultivation and release of his potentialities, and these should be integrated into a wholesome philosophy and purpose in living. He should see rich possibilities in his daily vocation, in his relationships as a citizen, in his family life, in his church and other organizational relations, and in general cultural interests. To all these, general education may make significant contributions at all age levels, and religious education is in part the spirit, attitudes, and values being stimulated in the whole process. The writer does not agree with those who would separate spiritual ends of the public school from those of the church and organized religion. The trend toward naturalism would do away with this unfortunate dualism and would unify life around great beliefs and purposes.

One trend in education which deserves special attention at this point is the tendency to short-cut the process of learning by a system of indoctrination. Certain ends are assumed to be so important that educators want them assured and attained without delay. For instance, democracy is taken as an ideal to be transmitted, and a set of techniques and verbalisms are organized to make it the accepted way of life. In order to secure a democracy, totalitarian methods are used; and the rights and needs of freedom of thought and judgment are ignored. If democracy is a desirable end, it will not be lost in a critical, creative process of education in which the perspective of history and analysis of alternatives are carefully considered. Vital democracy is not conformity to a set pattern of ideas or practices but rather free co-operative thinking and experimenting. There is yet much to be done to develop capacities and attitudes equal to the radical logic of democracy, and it will not be attained by merely talking emotionally about the ideals. Indoctrination is a reversion to the outgrown idea of education by direct transmission. It may be the tool of a totalitarian regime where obedient puppets are wanted, but it does not develop spiritual responses consonant with democratic ideals.

Recognizing, then, the essential spiritual qualities in good general education, what are the special problems of the religious quest, if there are any special ones not to be included in general education? The majority of people brought up on conventional religion would state the central topics for religious education as outlined in the seven objectives of the International Council of Religious Education: fostering a consciousness of God, experiencing Jesus Christ as Savior and Lord, interpreting the universe as a Christian, appreciating the Bible, being loyal to the church, developing a Christian social order, and attaining a Christlike character. As presented and dealt with by most Christian educators, these are matters of indoctrination. There is an attempt to secure certain ends without providing a body of experiences and opportunities for critical creative thinking which might make the ends meaningful and dynamic. In spite of the fact that every penny carries the slogan "In God we trust there is no agreement, among theologians or laymen, as to the concept of God. It is a vague term around which endless controversies center. Likewise, there is wide difference in interpretation of the life and teaching of Jesus, and the theological arguments about salvation and atonement are hopelessly involved. The phrase "Christian interpretation of the universe recalls the bitter fights between science and religion with the attempts to make some preconceived idea of God determine beliefs about the observable facts of the universe. Similarly, there is confusion about the other goals, with conflicting opinions as to the nature and importance of the Bible and the church and with radically different meanings for, and methods for attaining, a Christian social order and a Christlike character. All these objectives suggest important ends for religious education, but they imply indoctrination as the method for realizing them and ignore the learning process by which meanings grow, ideas are refined, and motives are aroused. They tend to make religion a conformity to patterns of verbal expression and vague loyalties rather than intelligent appreciations, growing insights, and satisfying commitments.

It is sometimes assumed that the first question of children will be theological, but this is not true. If they are in an atmosphere in which the term God is repeatedly used, they will want to know what God means. But when a child asks who made the sun or what makes the flowers grow, the needed answer is not in vague theological terms. And to take advantage of such questions to introduce the term God is not religious education.   Children need to understand the processes of life, to respect the wonderful, complex character of these processes and to feel the possibilities of becoming acquainted with them and of working with them. As they grow and as knowledge widens and deepens, they need to feel more and more at home in the universe, to sense their place and value in the total scheme of ongoing life, and to get satisfaction from asking questions and thinking with others on the interesting, though often perplexing, problems of life. In spite of the fact that the Hebrew-Christian varieties of religion have on the average been higher than most others, it should not seem necessary to set all religious ideas and values in terms of these traditions. As in general education, not only do we need acquaintance with prescientific religious concepts, the classical biblical ideas, and historical forms, but we also require investigation of why people believed as they did in olden days, what additional knowledge we have today of the world processes, what history has to tell us of the meanings and worth-while goals of living, and what the best judgments are in our own era.   Religion has always been functional when it has been vital, but it has not always had the same body of knowledge, social facts, and problems to deal with; and so it has been different in each situation where it has formulated theologies and practices for group use. Hence, it must remain a quest without authoritative and fixed concepts, institutions, or mores.

The common assumptions that religion deals with the "super-natural" and that truth is "revealed" must be subject to free critical inquiry. Neither term can be defined so that all who claim such belief agree on what is meant. What some call "supernatural" is simply an inference from incomplete knowledge of that which others call "natural." Both the supernaturalist and the naturalist live in the same world and have many common experiences, -and both seek as large fulfillment as possible of their lives. The naturalist may value the orderly creative forces of life and the spirit of love, justice, and dependability without either personifying them as God or assuming a divine being as portraying these characteristics. To some, religion is worship of an assumed God; to others it is an attempt to get an appreciation of the cosmic resources and to understand the inherent laws and possibilities of life. And as for revelation, naturalists believe that anything which may be "revealed" must be interpreted and understood in terms of the rest of life or it has no significance for them. Both concepts, "supernatural" and "revelation," lie in the field of emotional experiences, which have not been critically studied. To the naturalist and functionalist, religion cannot put a premium on the vague and not-yet-analyzed experiences of life without being discredited by persons accustomed to critical thinking. If experience teaches us that we live in a universe where there is unity, the basic truths of religion must be discoverable in the observable facts of life.

As people explore the possibilities of personal-social living, the gap between the growing ideal and the existing state of human affairs steadily widens. For some the religious solution is a miraculous intervention by an assumed deity and the perfect fulfillment in another world after death. For others the proof of spiritual realities is in their power to be realized in the present life-process. The achievement of social and economic justice, the establishment of peace and good will among men, the correction of crime tendencies, the refinement of sex, the mutual respect of persons for each other in the varied relationships of life, the enjoyment of the beauties and abundant privileges of a good world by everyone, and other ideals are being increasingly realized while the means for their further attainment are being sought. Religion is appreciation of the resources and laws of growth and commitment to a co-operative way of living, without any feeling of wanting a deity to reduce the responsibilities of intelligence.

To sum up the steps in the development of this quality of religion which we have called the quest, we present the following needed processes of religious education:

1. Answer the questions of inquiring children, youth, and adults by directing attention to the learning opportunities in formal and informal education, to the opportunities for direct observation of the processes of an orderly world, and to the possibilities of experimenting and evaluating with the best known ways of living, in seeking the basic meanings and worth of life.

2. Encourage critical and creative thinking, helping growing persons to find the secrets of progressively satisfying procedures in the everyday activities of co-operative living.

3. Help growing persons to get the perspective of history, to feel the slow growth of comprehensive spiritual values and the skills of religious living, and to be able to identify and to use the manifold privileges for personal-social enrichment.

4. Provide guidance by trained persons in the evaluation of ancient concepts and the development of religious ideas and practices so that the distinction may be appreciated between temporal forms and underlying realities.

5. Show how the functional interpretation of religion is in harmony with the quest of the ages and represents the pervasive and continuous spirit of living religion in all centuries.

6. Let the problems and fields of study in religious education be graded to the widening experience and maturing development of people, without confusing young children with theological abstractions and without prejudicing appreciations by indoctrinating methods of teaching.

7. Give frequent occasions for recognizing the progress in religious understanding and in the skills of living spiritually so that the quest may prove rewarding and revealing.

* * * * * * * * * *

Sophia L. Fahs

[From *Today's Children and Yesterday's Heritage: A Philosophy of Creative Religious Development* (Boston: Beacon Press, 1952), pp. 15-21.]

Nothing is so voluntary an affair as religion, in which, if the mind of the worshiper is averse to it, it is already destroyed and is not religion.

--

LACTANTIUS

THE RELIGIOUS BELIEFS which an individual makes his own undoubtedly influence his character development. But of even more profound influence than the beliefs themselves are the *ways* through which beliefs are acquired. It is here that the really vital issue is joined between the major divergent groups in religious education.

In one group religion is considered as something *given* to an individual by an authority other than himself, by an authority coming from the past--from revelation, from an inspired book, from a divine person, or from a divinely ordained church. Thus religion becomes a body of "affirmations" presented as "truths" to be understood, appreciated and accepted. When personally accepted, these "truths" become the object of one s faith and the focus of one's devotion. Certainty regarding such "truths" is thought to be especially important for young children who are considered incapable of thinking for themselves about such vital and difficult matters, yet who need the security that certainty can bring. It is said that their inborn but undeveloped consciences need to be empowered to choose the "good" rather than the "evil." By religion promulgated in this way characters are indeed molded.

The other group holds a less common and sharply different conception of religious development. For them beliefs regarding the universe and man's destiny in it should be the products of maturing emotional experiences, meditation and critical thought, and not assumptions with which to begin. Religion is, therefore, not a heritage which the child has a God-given right to receive, not something to be imparted to him by a teacher or a group. Rather it is regarded as a vital and healthy result of his own creative thought and feeling and experience as he responds to life in all its fullness.

Such a religion will develop slowly. The initial steps are largely emotional, exploratory and unorganized. Out of these early emotional beginnings the individual formulates a philosophy of life for himself. Influences from without and from the past affect the formation of such a religion; but the life-giving element is within the child and in his present experiences. Such a process of achieving religion never ceases. Full maturity is never attained. As the personality grows and changes so do the beliefs grow and change.

Thus we see that in one group religion is conceived of as a heritage received from the past and delivered with the stamp of authority. In the other its inspiration in the beginning and throughout the total span of life arises out of the natural needs and concerns of the individual who seeks a rich and satisfying life.

Although the contrast between these two points of view should not be exaggerated, neither should the difference be regarded lightly. For if one thinks of religion primarily in terms of something created by each individual, the first question to be asked is not: What has religion to give to a child? It is rather: How may a child contribute to his own religious growth? It is not: How does religion influence character development? Instead, the question of first importance is: How does character development influence the kind of religion a child makes his own? How is it possible for a child to build his own religion? Only when we understand the child's potentialities can we understand how we, his elders, may help or hinder him in gradually assuming responsibility for forming his religion.

Not only does the point of view one takes on this major issue determine the starting point, but also it affects continually the very nature of the processes of religious guidance, the goals sought, and the emotional atmosphere that is maintained between adults and children.

Since the conception of religion as a gift coming from the past to be handed on from one generation to another is such a dominant one in our society, it is important that we examine more carefully the effect of this point of view on the methods by which children have been taught religion, and the results that have accrued from it.

Ever since our forefathers first established our democracy on this continent, it has been assumed that each particular group or sect in our society should be responsible for transmitting its own religion to its own children. Each group, believing that it has the best to give, musters all its efforts to impart with persuasive power that which it proclaims as the truth. The attempt is made openly, and with general approval, to bind young children by personal loyalty to the religion of their fathers and to hold them in later life within the religious fold into which they were born.

In this approach, therefore, the beliefs characterizing each particular group are given a large emphasis in work with children. These beliefs are of two types, those that express the nature of God and man's obligations to him, and those which indicate what is "right" and what is "wrong" in man's conduct toward his fellow men. Of these two types, the beliefs pertaining to the existence and nature of God have usually been regarded in our Western culture as primary, being derived from a belief in God. The lack of belief in a God who ordains righteousness is commonly blamed for juvenile delinquency, the materialism of our civilization, and many other social evils.

This emphasis on belief in God is found in most Christian and Jewish literature for young children. The existence of God is assumed, however, rather than made the object of thoughtful study. Children are not expected to ask *why* people have believed that God is a reality. His existence and his attributes are taken for granted. Not only is God assumed, but the general system of moral ideas embodied in the Christian and Jewish heritage is also assumed as true and

"good."   God rewards the "good" and punishes the "bad."
Bible characters in most of the Bible story books for children
are either men who obeyed God's voice and were rewarded,
or who disobeyed and were punished. The fact that young
children have so little in their own experience by which to
judge critically what they are told is regarded usually as an
asset.   The early years are golden ones for such
indoctrination.

In common practice this emphasis is revealed in a type of
reasoning such as this: A small child cannot grasp an abstract
or cosmic thought of God. Since, however, "goodness" and
"love" are the most important aspects in "our best thought of
God," the God idea is made personal and concrete for the
child. In Christian circles young children are told stories of
Jesus as a man who was especially kind to children and to all
people in trouble. Then it is explained that Jesus is like God,
and that God is like Jesus; indeed, that the two are one and
the same.

God is commonly spoken of in religious literature as a
"loving Heavenly Father," who is different from flesh-and-
blood fathers since he is invisible, and his permanent home is
"heaven," a place vaguely located above the earth.   This
"Heavenly Father," although far away, is always near by. He
loves children and guards them so they need never be afraid;
however, he expects a great deal of children in return for his
love. He likes a "good" and "kind" child. He does not like
"bad" children.   Indeed, in much common conversation
between parents and children regarding God, he is presented
as prepared to inflict punishments on those who disobey their
parents, or who tell a lie. Bible stories are read or told to
young children in order that such beliefs and ideas of right
and wrong may be made more impressive. Although some of
the stories told contain accounts of miraculous happenings
which the parents or teachers themselves no longer regard as
records of facts, yet the children are told these stories
because they are in the Scriptures, and because the children
enjoy hearing them.

Let us examine the soundness of this point of view. What are the natural consequences in the emotional and intellectual development of the child?

To most children under six the world is filled with wonders for which they can give no reasonable explanation. Fairies, Santa Claus, witches, a snake that can talk, a man who can dam up the waters of a big sea merely by a command, are all believable. The story of angels singing in the sky over the birth of a baby is a wonderful fantasy for the child who has been told nothing about his own birth. A little child can imagine people being made well by a few spoken words. He can ask in prayer for a play-train and believe that God can produce the train in some magic way. Does the child himself not perform magic whenever he turns off the electric light or starts the radio by a twist of the fingers? To imagine the dead able to come back to life is a common fantasy among young children. Stories and tales of wonder are found in every religious culture, and are passed on to children as a part of their religious heritage. It is thought that to know the stories will in some way help to develop reverence, and will impress on children the desirability of pleasing God.

If these stories are told concretely in such a way that a young child can imagine the characters as real people in his present experience, and if he can identify himself emotionally with them, such methods may have great influence. But the question that should concern us is: What is the nature of the influence? will the child as a result of his faith in God feel more truly secure in his world or will his reasons for fear be increased? If a child looks upon floods, sickness, defeat in war, or death as forms of divine punishment (as they are so often presented in Biblical stories), will the fear of such punishments increase his desire or his power to be "good"? Or will the already rebellious child find a divine sanction for his own acts of aggression against those he dislikes? Will such stories give a child a sound understanding of his own capacities or will they tend to foster an illusion of strength by encouraging the expectation of some "special providence"? Will some children decide, as John did, that they too can

walk on water or do other impossible things because they
have accepted seriously the assurance of Jesus' power to
save? Or will Jesus simply become another superman in their
worlds of fantasy?

We do not doubt that the telling of Bible stories does mold
the thinking and feelings of young children. Our concern is
with the quality of the results. In just what ways are children
being influenced? What kinds of emotional needs are being
satisfied? Is the child's belief in magic being prolonged and
his growing-up retarded? Or do such methods really
sharpen his interest in the real nature of the universe and so
help him to grow toward maturity? Our experience has led
to the conclusion that there are much more promising ways
of introducing young children to religious feelings and beliefs
than through the early use of Bible-story books.

A second common way of introducing children to religion,
one that is equally authoritarian in type, is the way that
approaches beliefs indirectly through induction into religious
ceremonials. Little emphasis 15 given at first to the beliefs
implicitly in these ceremonials. In such groups, children are
taught to say the words of prayers and to perform acts in the
ceremonials before the ideas can be explained to them, and
sometimes almost before they can pronounce the words right.
Thus religion becomes, not so much a set of beliefs to be
upheld and accepted, as a pattern of group ceremonials into
which the child needs to be habit-trained. Religion becomes
something to be acted out in group rituals. Certain words are
to be said, certain postures taken, a certain vocabulary made
familiar. It is assumed the children in later years will clothe
the forms with meanings. In this kind of religious education
religion becomes a set of habit patterns to be followed, like
the daily bath or the rules of polite society.

What happens then in the immediate life experiences of
children so guided? Finding enjoyment in performing acts for
which the child can see no clear reason must lead him to
focus attention on adult approval and the pleasure of formal
participation rather than on the meanings beneath these
externals. Surely neither words nor acts that are without
meaning to a child can really nourish his life. This is an

effective method of tying children emotionally to their particular cultural patterns, without their feeling a need to examine the reasons for such patterns.

And what happens to the child as the years move on, as he finds that other groups have different ceremonies and believe differently? He cannot but equate the external words and rituals with his religion. If he does so, then religion becomes something that separates one group from another, rather than something that binds humanity together by means of deeply felt universal experiences underneath varying forms. Furthermore, children so taught will tend to think of religion as something unique to their particular ethnic group, something inherited from their particular ancestors and peculiar to their culture. Their own religion will naturally seem the best. Such children are likely to feel no more responsibility for the nature of their religion than they feel for the lands and money they may inherit.

* * * * * * * * *

*Understanding Trends in Protestant Education
in the Twentieth Century*

Harrison S. Elliott

[From *Can Religious Education Be Christian?* (New York: The Macmillan Company, 1940), pp. 316-21.]

Subject matter in such an experience-centered process is recognized as the record and interpretation of significant experience in the area under consideration or as data pertinent to understanding or solving the immediate problem, to be understood and used in its bearing upon the situation of the individual or the group. The Bible is recognized as a record of experience in meeting life's situations with significant insights as to the meaning of life and religion, indeed the most significant record of religious experience available. On the one hand, the purpose in the use of the Bible is to enable children and young people and adults to relive this experience, to recapture it imaginatively so that it does not consist of facts to be learned or verses to be memorized, but becomes alive in the present. In this way, their experience is widened and enriched. On the other hand, the purpose is to use this experience of the past to give help in meeting present situations, particularly to bring perspective and emphasis and point of view for current decisions and attitudes.

From this viewpoint, the experiences of prayer and worship do not take place alone, or even chiefly, in formal practices; but they represent the dominating spirit and attitude of this experience process, as individuals and groups seek to find the will of God for their lives and the resources of God for their endeavors, and as they evaluate their conduct on the basis of what they have discovered to be God's purpose and will in human life. Indeed, the so-called formal practices of prayer and worship are seen to have meaning and vitality only as they are alternations from life activity and are integrally related to life situations.

An experience-centered educational process does not imply lack of conviction. It only indicates how convictions are held. Convictions represent what seem to individuals or groups to be best. They act as if those convictions were final, but at the same time they take toward their action a critical attitude and seek ways of improving it. The two are not inconsistent. A physician acts on whatever he already knows with a confidence that has elements of finality, and yet he is continually searching for improvements in his theory and practice. So standards and practices which have been arrived at through the educational process should be followed with convictions, but should not be considered as rigidly fixed. They should be held as hypothetical and tentative, not in the sense that one cannot act because he is not sure, but in the truer sense that they are to be "tested and confirmed and latered through consequences affected by acting upon them."

An experience-centered educational process is inconsistent, however, with positions dogmatically and finally held. This is the source of much of the opposition to religious education and is also the cause of a conflict within education itself. There has often been a tendency for each religious faith to consider its own the only true religion. This results not only in the unwillingness to learn from other faiths, but also in the practice of branding them as false and untrue. Under these circumstances the followers of each faith feel the necessity of defending and propagating their own faith as the true religion. The search for truth is turned into dogmatic defense and counter-defense of a particular set of truths. Divisions arise and the fellowship of a true educational process is at an end. Religious education becomes a means for indoctrinating children and youth in a particular set of Christian interpretations or the propaganda by which others are influenced to accept that particular set of dogmas as the only true faith.

Religious leaders are not the only individuals with dogmatic certainty. Those who are at the extreme right in social and political outlook and wish to maintain the *status quo*, and those who have moved to the extreme left and wish to overthrow the existing order are often as dogmatic in their certainty as to the final right of their beliefs as are some of the followers of religion. Those at the right wish to use education to maintain the *status quo* and they oppose free discussion of current problems as zealously as they do the direct teaching of radical notions. Those at the extreme left would like to use education for the propagation of their proposed theories and they also are opposed to free consideration of these problems. Thus, a true educational process is being challenged both from the extreme right and the extreme left. It is not surprising to find that those of a religious outlook who move to a dogmatically held extreme left in economic and political theory should at the same time move to a dogmatically held extreme right in religious faith, for the extreme right in religion and the extreme left in economics and politics are often alike in dogmatic certainty. The conflict then is not alone between authoritarian religion and experimental education. It is rather a more fundamental cleavage between those of dogmatic certainty in ethical and religious beliefs, and those who take the experimental attitude toward life and who are convinced that ethical standards and goals of endeavor as well as religious beliefs are worked out by the same educational process as the means for their attainment. A true educational process is denied as soon as education is made the servant of any dogmatism, whether in religion or in any other area. The freedom of individuals and of groups to search for and find their own meaningful interpretations of life and destiny is important in religious education which is Christian. This liberty is in line with the spirit of the New Testament. It was a cardinal principle of the Reformation. It is true to the scientific spirit and method. It is that which gives Christian experience its vitality.

The issues in regard to religious education center in the source of authority. Those with an authoritarian approach seek to find authority for their interpretations outside of human responsibility in some direct revelation of God. Those with an educational approach recognize that while God has not left himself without witness, man has not been given any direct revelation of the meaning of these manifestations. He has been left to discover these manifestations and to make his own interpretations of them. It is true that man has by his own efforts produced nothing. His very capacity to take responsibility in his world is given him in his native equipment, and the resources upon which he depends he finds in his world. But it is also true that he is dependent for the development of his own capacities and for the discovery and utilization of these resources upon human responsibility and effort. Much of his learning has been "trial and error." True education of the social type represents conscious and effective ways by which human beings have met situations, have made decisions, have discovered and utilized available resources, and thus have taken responsibility in their world. Education is not something which is confined to the school. It is the fundamental method open to man for solving the problems of his world. It is the process used wherever significant responsibility is taken by man, whether in personal decisions and relations, in family life, community relations, or economic and political affairs. It is the basis for the conviction that individual growth and social progress are no longer at the mercy of circumstances, but become a possibility though not an inevitability. Therefore the source of authority is in the educational process itself. In saying this, there is recognition of the fact that it is only by such a process that man can determine what to do or can discover on what he may and must depend.

Trust, however, can be placed in an educational process only when it reaches a genuine religious level. Such a process is controlled by inclusive and even ultimate goals and purposes beyond the private welfare of any individual or group, and is grounded in discovery and utilization of the resources on which man's life depends. The source of authority for the Christian is in that educational process which is guided by Christian purposes and is grounded on the Christian's confidence. The contribution of the Christian religion to reverent human responsibility is not realized when the emphasis is limited to a sense of guilt for failure and to an offer of forgiveness for sin. What is needed is both confidence and direction for a different kind of responsibility from that which has brought defeat. An experience-centered

and socially organized educational process would seem to
furnish the medium for the utilization of these positive
contributions of Christian faith and experience. There is full
recognition of finite limitations and of the human possibilities
of evil as well as of good, and there is realistic appraisal of
the tragic seriousness of the human problem; but at the same
time there is integral in such an educational process what
seems to have been Jesus' confidence in the unrealized
possibilities even of plain and humble persons and groups.
While it is dominated by the Christian emphasis on the worth
of persons and upon mutual respect and brotherly relations
between them, it is centered in family, school, church,
community, and other corporate groupings where the choices
and responsibilities are intimately bound up with the social
groups of which they are a part. Therefore, the goal is truly
social, for it is that approximation which is possible to human
beings in their social arrangements of the Kingdom of God in
which love is manifested in all social relationships.
Confidence in the success of these human endeavors is based
upon the Christian belief in the limitless resources of God
which are available to individuals and groups who meet the
conditions for their release. Thus, Christian faith and
experience are integrally related to an educational process
which is Christian.

If confidence is to be placed in the educational process, the
Christian purpose and confidence must be more than a matter
of intellectual assent. It is only as individuals and groups
have been captured by the possibilities of love made manifest
in Christ, as the goal of the Kingdom of God has become the
dominating purpose of their lives, and as fellowship with God
has become an actual experience, that the educational
process can be trusted. There is hope of the beginning and
the growth of such living experience when individuals join
with their fellows in the enterprises of God on earth.

* * * * * * * * * *

It was only a matter of time that the once vital progressive
liberal movement which had dominated the thinking of

religious educators in the first part of the twentieth century would, for all intents and purposes, yield to the theological pressures of neo-orthodoxy

---

Notes

[1] Hartshorne and May, <u>Studies in Deceit</u> (New York, 1928).

The Rise of the "Theological" Era

Smith, Miller, Sherrill, Wyckoff, Nelson

With the rise of Hitler's Nazi Germany, and with the subsequent neo-orthodox theological response, the progressive-liberal era in religious education all but came to an uneventful end. The attempt to relate the neo-orthodox theological perspective(s) to *Christian* education *(religious* education as a term declined during this era because of its overt lack of a Christocentric focus) gave rise to a robust and fruitful movement especially in the second half of the twentieth century. Named by some the new "theological" era of the century, nothing could be more misleading. For the progressive-liberal era was also fundamentally a theological era; neo-orthodoxy simply named the theological/educational task differently--often fundamentally differently!--than did the liberal theological era.

No single figure so bluntly or so forcefully stated the theological differences between liberalism and neo-orthodoxy than did Shelton Smith. A much loved faculty member at Duke who died in 1987, Smith wrote *Faith and Nurture* as a direct response to Elliott's *Can Religious Education Be Christian?* While it is doubtful that Smith had any other interest than expunging *nurture* from the Christian educational lexicon, the title *does* set up the problematic--faith vs. nurture. Functionally, Smith influenced a whole generation of Christian educational theorists.

D. Campbell Wyckoff stands as the single most articulate spokesperson of the relationship of neo-orthodox theology and education. Known widely for his thoughtful work in curriculum theory and design, Wyckoff stands alone in his ability to draw insight from a *wide* range of disciplinary data, and then to relate them to the "gospel." His method has withstood the test of time and praxis.

Randolph Crump Miller was one of the first to clearly articulate that the "clue" to Christian education's theory and practice was theology. A communicator in the best sense, it is doubtful that a "theological era" would have been recognized on the popular level without his direct and applicable statements.

Lewis Joseph Sherrill made contributions to the field of Christian education on many grounds--history, curriculum, psychology. But it is this last area, psychology, that marks Sherrill as unique among his neo-orthodox colleagues. For he was the foundational spokesperson for the relationship of psychology, theology, and education.

C. Ellis Nelson developed an understanding of community-based communication that has not yet been surpassed in Christian educational theory. The relationship of faith, culture, and values was given coherence and depth by this central figure.

The neo-orthodox movement in Christian education, now in serious decline, was informed by some of the brightest and best minds in Protestantism. It must be remembered, however, that all members of this movement stood on the research and findings of those of the previous theological era--the progressive-liberal movement in religious education. While the religious education and Christian education movements were fundamentally opposed on *theological* grounds, there was more *educational* agreement than might first meet the eye.

* * * * * * * * * *

Shelton Smith
(1941)

[From *Faith and Nurture* (New York: Charles Scribner's Sons, 1941), pp. 42-53.]

This emphasis on the value of persons has become almost an obsession with the modern religious educator. Being his stock-in-trade, he injects the theme into practically every educational discussion. Whether he undertakes to express the nature of the Kingdom of God or that of democracy, he is almost certain to come round sooner or later--and usually sooner--to the "personality principle." This is especially true of those Christian liberals who stress what they term "democratic religion."[1]   Yet this interest in democratic religion has tended in some circles to obscure the divine ground of human value. This may be seen in two types of emphasis in modern religious thought. One of these is the emphasis on what is spoken of as the principle of the "infinite value" of human personality. In support of this principle appeal has often been made to the Biblical passage, "What shall it profit a man if he shall gain the whole world and lose his own life?" It is clearly loose exegesis, however, to say that this passage supports the idea of the infinite value of personality. From this text one may claim only that persons are of more worth than the "whole world." As between the world of things and the world of persons, persons are, to be sure, superior in value to things. One may ask, "Of how much more value is a man than a sheep?" without implying that man is a being of absolute worth. From the standpoint of Christian faith there seems to be no ground on which to say that human personality is a value of "final worth."[2]   For to ascribe final worth to persons is in effect to deny Christianity's claim that man is a contingent creature. The secular humanist may legitimately attribute final or absolute value to persons; for to him there is no being beyond man himself. Christian faith, however, cannot do this without sacrificing an essential element in its doctrine of man. For it is the Christian faith that man is a theonomous being. This means man is not autonomous or final, but derives his meaning and value from his relation to God, the highest value.   When, therefore, the principle of respect for personality is carried to the length of endowing persons with supreme worth, then the Christian conception of human value is perverted. The way is then opened for a subtle deification of humanity. And this, in turn, starts a trend toward the kingdom of man as a substitute for the Kingdom of God.

There is a second type of emphasis that likewise threatens to obscure the divine ground of the value of persons. It arises out of a certain type of social interpretation of the origin and nature of personality. Under the influence of social psychology, it has become a commonplace to conceive the emergence of personal selves in terms of social interaction. Self-consciousness and social consciousness, it is said, not only arise together; the experience of being a self is *per se* an experience of other selves.[3]   Thus "my self-consciousness is social consciousness."[4]   Some thinkers, following George H. Mead, even go so far as to say that the self is purely the result of an interactive process between the human organism and the natural world.

This tendency of thought has greatly influenced the social theory of liberal religious education. With it there has emerged a definite tendency to equate the value of man with his value to humanity. Since persons are said to be the locus of supreme value, and since values are *per se* social values, human value lies in the fact that man is a member of the Great Society. Personality is thus sacred to society. Persons not only realize themselves in and through society; the Great Society is itself the norm by which their value must finally be measured. But when the values of persons are thus measured exclusively in social or human terms, it is obvious that persons lose their transcendent meaning and value. With their transcendent value denied or obscured, the way is therefore opened to subordinating persons to whatever social system may become dominant. It is no surprise that the complete socialization of human value should be followed by some sort of dictatorship, whether of the Left or of the Right.

(b) There is a second tendency that is closely related to the first. It is the tendency to identify religion with the process of the discovery of the ethical meaning and worth of persons. Since persons are of supreme worth, the educative process in religion must, it is said, center in the experience of self-realizing persons.

In his *Psychology of Religion*, George A. Coe writes: "Religion is the discovery of persons."[5] In the history of religion, it is said, man has gradually and progressively discovered himself. Self-discovery is inseparably social, since persons realize themselves only in and through social interaction. The mark of the growth of religion and of the discovery of man alike is thus social integration. The wider the social integration, the higher will be religion and the more meaningful will be man. The process of social integration is dynamic and never stops, else religion becomes arrested and thereby obstructs cultural and ethical evolution. The creative center of this process of continuous integration is man in process of personal-social self-realization. Man is discovering himself, it is said, through the reintegration of his wants in terms personal-social self-realization. "And this is religion."[6]

Involved in this view that religion is the discovery of persons is another idea that must not be overlooked. It is the idea that, in the order of religious apprehension, man first discovers fresh values in human relations and then projects them into the nature of ultimate reality.[7] Thus new insights into the ethical character of God are dependent upon new and more radical adventures in the ethical relations of persons. Harrison S. Elliott implies this when he says that "God is found as individuals find themselves in the great cooperative enterprises for human progress."[8] A psychological analysis of the history of religious evolution is supposed to support the claim that fresh insight into the character of God follows rather than precedes cultural evolution. Faith in God "is social valuation asserting itself as objectively valid."[9] "It is a perfectly safe assertion," says Coe, "that men first attributed ethical love to the divine be~g after they had experienced it among themselves."[10]

Now it is our claim that this general emphasis has tended to obscure the theocentric meaning of the Kingdom. When religion is conceived as the process of the discovery of persons, it inevitably follows that the educational process of the Church will concern itself with the interhuman relations of persons. From this it follows logically that the integrating core of the curriculum of the Church will be "social relations."[11] It is usually assumed, of course, that the divine is in some sense immanent in these social relations, and that under certain conditions of fellowship the qualities of the divine will emerge.[12]

But as a matter of fact this mode of approach has not resulted in a primary emphasis on God at all. On the contrary, persons as an interactive community have been made central. There is an implied assumption that contact with God may be made only indirectly through social relations. Thus Edwin E. Aubrey comments in respect of a conference of religious educators: "It was curious that no reference was made in the discussions of religious education to the problem of man's direct contact with God; and the tendency was to identify this in some way with social contacts."[13]

Any such view involves distinct peril for Christian faith, and consequently peril for Christian nurture. To be sure, one's contact with God is stimulated and enriched by social community. But if any one should assume that there can be no sort of contact with God except through other persons, then he assumes something which involves an infinite regress of relations which either denies or obscures the reality of God. Any such view, furthermore, involves a denial that man may experience contact with God in and through the processes of the world of nature. It involves also a denial of God as transcendent of human creatures.

There is a further weakness in the view that religion is primarily the discovery of persons. Not only does it tend to equate the experience of God with the experience of social community, but it tends to identify experience of God with a certain mode or quality of human striving. In his autobiographical essay, George A. Coe says: "Religion is not something added to the functions that make a man a man, but something already within these functions *when they are intensely pursue*. To be religious is as natural as it is to be in dead earnest about anything."[14]

Implicit in this point of view are two dangers. The first is religious subjectivity. The principle of intensity of effort contains in itself no criterion as to what makes any particular function or experience religious. For one may pursue energetically any sort of goal, whether good or bad. Even if one should combine the principle of intensity of pursuit with the process of the discovery of persons, the key to what makes a given function religious is still subjective and obscure.

The second danger is activism. From the view that religion is a quality of experience that arises through intense effort, it follows that Christian nurture will concern itself less with the Divine Initiative than with human striving. This is precisely what has happened. The idea of progressive religious education is rooted in the assumption that religious experience emerges where self-realizing persons creatively adjust themselves to their natural and social world. On this basis the creative center is located in self-striving man, who is conceived as the builder of the Kingdom. To be sure, the reality of the Kingdom of God is not denied; nevertheless, it is regarded as chiefly the result of human achievement. Thus the source of the Kingdom has become in effect anthropocentric.

Before leaving this topic we must examine the notion that persons first achieve insights and values within human

relations and only thereafter project them into the character
of God.[15]   Particular values attributed to God are, in this
view, a derivative of social evolution.   It is assumed,
therefore, that new apprehensions of the divine follow social
re-evaluation of values.   Thus it follows that new values in
God await new valuations among men.   A new insight into
God's nature cannot be had, it is said, "until we experience a
new social order in operation."[16]

We must frankly question the basic assumption that under-
lies this notion. That the history of religion supports it seems
doubtful.   To be sure, the rise of religion does reflect
changing conceptions of God.   For example, God was
conceived as a tribal being at one stage of Israel's culture and
as a universal being at another.   But does this fact warrant
one in assuming that a higher estimate of the character of
God could not arise until antecedent reconstruction in the
social culture had first achieved it? Apparently not. For in
that case the belief that God desired universal peace, for
example, would have been inconceivable in the days of
Micah, since at that time a world society had not yet realized
universal peace.

There is, to be sure, a vital connection between human
relations and fellowship with God.   An ancient Christian
writer reminds us of this fact, when he says: "He that sayeth,
I love God, and hateth his brother, is a liar." This passage,
however, lends no support to the notion that the quality of
love must first be achieved exclusively in human relations
before it can be applied to the nature of God. Indeed, great
religious prophets have always transcended the experiences
and insights of the social culture in which they grew up.[17] It
is unrealistic to assume that the religious insights of an Isaiah,
for   example,   were   merely   social   achievements   and
evaluations projected into the character of the universe.
Isaiah's vision had crucial consequences for the social scene,
but that vision did not itself grow out of an already
reconstructed social order. In his experience of a holy God,

Isaiah recognized that he was a man of unclean lips, and it was on the basis of this experience that he was able to make the social evaluation, "and I dwell among a people of unclean lips."

The point of this should be clear. Those who would have us believe that new insights into the divine nature can be achieved only after they have been realized within human relations, not only deny the most characteristic aspect of prophetic religion; they invert the order of moral insight. They thus weaken religious insight at the very point where they seek to awaken it. It cannot be denied, of course, that social crises precipitate serious reflection, and that this mood predisposes the sensitive ear to hear "what the Spirit saith unto the churches." Nor can it be denied that man's ideals serve as a medium through which to envisage the moral character of God. Such truths may be recognized, however, without one's needing to conclude that new religious insight can emerge only from an already achieved new social order.

(c) A third sort of tendency that we shall examine briefly is connected with the idea of sovereignty. Either explicitly or implicitly the value of persons is usually assumed to be the ultimate ground and dynamic of the democratic state. We have already seen that liberal religion also makes the value of persons one of its most creative principles. Thus both democracy and religion are one in emphasizing the essential dignity and worth of persons. In this respect, at least, these two interests are reciprocal in modern culture.[18]

It is of interest to observe that, concurrent with this emphasis on the dignity and worth of persons, there has been a tendency to modify the idea of divine sovereignty. Democratic religion, it has been urged, cannot fulfil its true meaning until it has brought about a democratic theology.[19] "Must not Christians," asks George A. Coe, "think of God as being within human society in the democratic manner of working, helping, sacrificing, persuading, co-operating, achieving?"[20]

This point of view finds a significant application in Bower's theory of religious education. In his view God is not only experienced in the fellowship of group participation; God is Himself a democratic sharer in the group process. "As a member of the community," says Bower, "God shares in the ideals, purposes, and decisions of the group, *as do its other members.* Contrariwise, the decisions of the group are made with reference to what are believed to be the ideals and purposes of the Supreme Member. In such a situation prayer as communion between himself and God becomes as normal as communion between himself and other members of the group."[21]

This democratic interpretation of God's relation to men has served important ends. As over against a concept of God as one who stands aloof from the human struggle, who rules by arbitrary decree, and who manipulates persons as mechanical puppets, the democratic idea of God is certainly to be preferred. But insofar as the democratic idea of God obscures the fact that God is wholly sovereign in His Kingdom, and that man is utterly dependent upon God, it must be regarded as defective. There is reason to believe that the true meaning of   divine   sovereignty has been obscured in modern culture. The root of this obsuration may be found in modern religious thought as well as in democratic theory.

It is generally agreed that the locus of sovereignty in modern political democracy is in "we, the people." In the democratic state, says Coe, the sovereign "is neither a god nor the surrogate of a god. ... The sovereign is just ourselves when we co-operatively insist upon providing for ourselves what we want."[22] And this "is the ultimate meaning of the separation of the church from the state."[23] The implication of this point of view almost startles one. It seems to say in effect that whenever persons jointly determine to pursue their self-chosen ends, there is no sovereignty beyond themselves by which they need feel bound. Human sovereignty, in this view, is primordial and self-sufficient. "Actual, living sovereignty ... is wholly within the flux of experience; ... it is in continuous creation and re-creation, even within ourselves."[24]

If this be the ultimate meaning of the separation of the democratic state from the Church, then it cannot be doubted that the theory of the modern democratic state does obscure the truth of divine sovereignty. If the Kingdom of God be truly sovereign over every social community, the democratic state included, then it cannot be admitted that divine sovereignty is wholly within the flux of human experience. On the other hand, when the ultimate meaning of sovereignty is wholly identifiable with the inner meaning of the fellowship of persons, the only sovereignty that can be recognized is human sovereignty.

Liberal Christianity has also had a part in obscuring the principle of the sovereignty of God in His Kingdom. This is reflected, for example, in the liberal's emphasis on divine immanence. If religious orthodoxy sometimes tended to deny all continuity between God and man, liberalism has tended to overemphasize continuity. The doctrine of immanence afforded liberal religious thought a basis upon which to conceive of man as being essentially divine in the depth of his being, and therefore as containing within himself the essential principle of his own worth and government. In this lies the main source of human dignity and of self-determination.

* * * * * * * * * *

Randolph Crump Miller
(1950)

[From *The Clue to Christian Education* (New York: Charles Scribner's Sons, 1950), pp. 1-17.]

There is something new in the theory and practice of Christian education. It is coming out of parents' and teachers' meetings in terms which they do not often understand; it is being expressed by pastors in their dissatisfaction with both the older methods of teaching and the newer and progressive methods; it is being illustrated by the demand for new lesson materials, by the experiments being made among the educational leaders of the various denominations, and by the increased cooperation between home and Church.

It is hard to put one's finger on the exact problem, because the difficulty now confronting us is being expressed primarily in negative terms. There is increasing dissatisfaction with the content-centered teaching which is still prevalent, and there is also widespread distrust of the so-called life-centered teaching. This vagueness of analysis is further illustrated by the enthusiasm with which new tricks have been tried: There are no answers to the basic problem in novel teaching methods, in the use of motion pictures and other visual aids, or in expanded time for the education of both children and adults, important as these things are.

Some of the difficulties of the older materials were overcome by turning to the experience of the learner as a basic element in educational procedure. The earlier methods had been catechetical, or ungraded, or Bible centered, with no thought for the religious needs and experiences of the pupils. To get away from this emphasis on content, it was decided to begin at the "growing edge" of the learner and lead him through his increased interests and insights toward a fuller and richer Christian life. Too often, the procedure was reversed, so that "a little child shall lead them" not to the deepest truths of Christian living, but to the vagaries of childhood or the mutual interchange of ignorance of high school students in a bull session or the prejudices of ill-informed adults. As a matter of fact, the main goal of education was lost sight of just as much in life-centered as in content-centered teaching, for the goal of all education is quite clearly to learn "truth," and there is no easy way to acquire or impart "truth."

This points to the fundamental weakness in practically all educational theory: a failure to grasp the purpose of Christian education and to impart Christian truth.   "Ye shall know the truth, and the truth shall make you free, we are told; but when the emphasis has been on truth, there has been no method adequate to impart it; and when there have been effective methods, there has been no fundamental truth to guide them.   Our philosophy of educational method has been sound at the expense of theology, while both true and false theologies have been presented without the methods to bring them to life in the experiences of the learners.

Let us illustrate this thesis: It is true that a little child learns primarily through activity, and that what he sees or touches or smells is of greater significance than what he hears. He can learn great lessons about God because he can see, touch, or smell a flower or a doll or a baby. But too often he achieves romantic and unrealistic views of natural processes because the interpretation is not fundamentally either scientific or Christian, and as a result he will have to unlearn this meaning of nature as he grows older.

A child in the fifth grade may spend a great deal of time making a relief map of Palestine. This is an enjoyable occupation, and he will be able to show the routes which Jesus followed from Nazareth to Jerusalem, and he will understand the deadness of the Dead Sea and the sudden storms on the Lake of Galilee. Too often such knowledge will bring him no closer to seeing what it means to accept Jesus as the Christ, and while his geographical insights may have improved greatly and he may have become a quite adequate map maker, he will be no farther along the road to becoming a Christian. This type of worthwhile and exciting activity will keep him occupied, and the methodology is fundamentally sound, but unless "something new has been added," it will result in an actual stoppage of Christian growth.

The examples on the other side are equally frustrating. There was a time when the same Bible story was taught to each age-group and all learners were treated alike, because, if the story were in the Bible it had to be taught some day. While it is generally admitted that this is impossible today even in the smallest ungraded Church school, there are still many hang-overs in educational circles. First grade children are expected to recite and understand the Apostles' creed. Uniform lessons are still among the best sellers of Church school materials. The catechism is still taught in terms of set questions and answers. Some parents and Church school leaders are disturbed when their children do not learn by rote Bible verses which are so many meaningless jumbles to the youngsters, although it is recognized that the right use of memorization is valuable.

The dissatisfaction with the dilemmas has led the writers of Church school courses to seek a new solution. They have not worked out a theory, but there is in their efforts a hint to the proper theory. The newest Bible courses have not been placed simply on a problem-solving level. It has been discovered that the Bible is not only the source of potential solution to many problems, but that it has within it the power to suggest new questions to which it has the answer. So it has been that courses have been worked out which make full use of the specific problems of a particular age-group, but which lead them also into the mystery of the Bible as something worth knowing in itself. The same thing has been done with Church history, so that whereas historical processes and events are understood in terms of modern problems, they are also comprehended within the framework of the situations actually facing the historical actors and writers. Clues to a solution of the problem have also been provided by the writers of courses on worship, for it has been discovered that worship is the experience-centered method par excellence for educational purposes, that worship is an activity of one who knows himself to be in the presence of

God, to whom the worshiper brings his own difficulties and in the presence of whom he finds solace and power and blessing. Courses on Christian ethics have also stumbled on this same truth, that the central beliefs of the Christian tradition are relevant to present-day living.

I

But the insights of such discoveries, important as they are, do not quite get at the heart of the problem. The major task of Christian education today is to discover and impart the relevance of Christian truth. The one missing topic in most educational schemes today is theology, and in theology properly interpreted lies the answer to most of the pressing educational problems of the day. The new element in educational theory is the discovery of the organic relation between doctrine and experience, between content and methods, between truth and life.

Now before this is misunderstood, two things must be said. This is not a plea to return to a content-centered curriculum, for it is perfectly clear that an emphasis on content as an end in itself leads to verbalism, whereby the learner repeats the words but is not concerned with the meaning. That is like trying to Christianize a parrot, and success cannot be achieved by that method. In the second place, it is not a desire to return to indoctrination, for indoctrination implies a kind of authority which is consistent with controlled propaganda rather than with the growth of individuals in the Christian way of life.

But if neither content nor indoctrination provides the clue, how can theology be at the center of the curriculum? The answer is that theology is not at the center. The center of the curriculum is a twofold relationship between God and the learner. The curriculum is both God-centered and experience-centered. Theology must be prior to the curriculum! Theology is "truth-about-God-in-relation-to-man." In order to place God and man at the center of the

Christian educational method, we must have adequate knowledge of the nature and working of both God and man, and of God's relationships to particular pupils.

For example, it would be possible to work out a sound curriculum based on the Apostles' creed (assuming that the creed is true in so far as it may be proved by Scripture and made meaningful in experience). But the creed would be placed back of the curriculum rather than in it. It would be introduced into the curriculum in terms of the relevance of Christian truth to the experiences and capacities of the learners, until at the proper level it could be studied as a summary of truths which are relevant to Christian living today. Most of us would not think of this as an adequate curriculum, unless it were enriched by the many implications of the creed (and if the space of time indicated by the punctuation between "Mary, suffered" were taken seriously, we could teach the life of Christ), but there would be a depth of meaning and a richness of experience provided by even so inadequate a curriculum which are lacking in most modern approaches to Christian education.

The task of Christian education is not to teach theology but to use theology as the basic tool for bringing learners into the right relationship with God in the fellowship of the Church. We have tried the Bible as a tool, and have ended up with some knowledge of the Bible but with no basic principles for using it properly. It is true that Holy Scripture is the basic authority for theology, but it is also evident that theology is a guide to the meaning of the Bible. Theology provides the perspective for all subjects, and yet all subjects are to be taught in terms of the interests and capacities of the learners in their relationship to God and to their fellow man.

When we say that truth is the underlying principle of the curriculum, this does not mean that we can be dogmatic about it. We need to recognize the great varieties of concepts held to be true by various individuals and denominations calling themselves Christian, and then to grant that our teachers will be bound to a theological system in terms of their own loyalty and freedom. The degrees of authority and freedom will vary from communion to communion, and from congregation to congregation within a communion, so that the writer of lesson materials and the teacher of a class will still have to use their own intelligence in making selections of theological tools for religious instruction.

There is great danger in this approach, as we have said, for it opens the door to the emphasis on content at the expense of Christian growth, and it could bring us back to the old idea of indoctrination, but the safeguard against this error is the insistence that there is a proper relationship between content and method. It is this relationship which needs further investigation. If we are right in our assumption that theology lies back of the curriculum and is to be introduced into it in the light of the "growing edge" of the learner, we need to understand the relation of theology to Christian living at the various age-levels, and this involves what is even more fundamental: the relevance of theology for all of life.

A person's behavior is guided by his deepest convictions, for what he believes in his inmost self determines his actions. His motivations are organically related to this theology. He may hold these concepts consciously or unconsciously. He may behave in a way foreign to a creed which he deceives himself into thinking he accepts, and thus may indicate that his basic drives are other than what he professes (and the hypocrite is one who professes one set of beliefs and acts according to another set). The complexity of his personality and the -confusion of his motives may blur the picture of the relation between his beliefs and his behavior. But when the principle of this relationship is applied consistently and with due regard for all the factors, it will be discovered that the beliefs which are habitually held (and thus taken seriously even when one is not conscious of them) are the normal bases for action.

If this be true, it is of the greatest significance for Christian education. It explodes both the traditional view and the progressive one, for the traditional view insists that beliefs be accepted within the framework of a certain vocabulary regardless of their relevance, while the progressive view ultimately is reduced to the solving of a problem within the frame ~f reference of that problem and without regard to the wider cosmic or metaphysical point of view. If theology comes into the foreground of Christian teaching, there is great danger that beliefs will be held which are not part of one's basic personality pattern, whereas if theology is disregarded there is no sense of ultimate purpose.

Theology in the background; faith and grace in the foreground might well be the slogan for this new point of view. The center of the educational process is neither theology nor the individual learner. The purpose of Christian education is to place God at the center and to bring the individual into the right relationship with God and his fellows within the perspective of the fundamental Christian truths about all of life--a Christian view of the universe, a Christian view of God who is known in experience and in the historical process, a knowledge of Jesus Christ who is to be accepted as Lord and Savior, a view of man which actually accounts for the experiences of damnation and salvation, an acceptance of the Church as a people-church in a covenant relationship with God, and the experience of the learner in terms of the realities underlying these concepts. When such a relationship between content and method is achieved, theology becomes relevant to Christian living, and education is almost synonymous with evangelism. Evangelism has often been ignored or misunderstood in modern educational circles, but its essential purpose can never be ignored if Christian education is to remain a vital force in the life of the Church. To evangelize is to confront men with Jesus Christ, so that they will put their trust in God through him, and by the power of the Holy Spirit live as Christ's disciples in the fellowship of the Church.

The person who by faith comes to this position is said to be integrated. The integration of the personality which is the goal of religious instruction can never be achieved in terms of ideals alone (as in character education), or of beliefs alone (as in indoctrination), or of social adjustment alone (as in much modern psychiatry). Just at the point where Christianity is unique, its educational philosophy and its methods have fallen down. The weakness of the good man who lacks religion is that his personality is centered on ideals and he becomes like the Pharisee in Jesus' parables. The charge against religious fanatics is that they know Bible verses and creeds, but have little insight into the meaning of Christlikeness. The trouble with many who have made good social adjustments is that they lack the divine discontent which is the only motivation for making a better world.

There must be a deeper integration. Theology, in so far as it represents truth, points in the direction of a Christian answer, which is that Christian integration lies in the relationship between God and man. It is the integration which results from a deep and abiding personal relationship between God and man. It flows from a right religious adjustment which is a basic process of living. It is more than intellectual or emotional or volitional activity, for it involves the total personality in relation to~the ultimate reality, who is God. The human integration of a child does not evolve from his idea of his parents. It comes from his relationship with his parents. So also, his religious integration does not come primarily from his idea of God. It comes from his personal relationship with God.

It is central to the educational theory of these chapters to recognize the radical nature of Christian integration. Modern studies in psychology point toward the same emphasis: a man's integration is in terms of the organic relation between himself and his environment, not in terms of ideas or values but in terms of the situation in which he finds himself. It is

Christian theology which adds a further element, that central in the Christian's environment is the living God and that the frame of reference for Christian living is he in whom we live and move and have our being. The Epistle to the Ephesians describes it as "reaching maturity, reaching the full measure of development which belongs to the fullness of Christ-- instead of remaining immature, blown from our course and swayed by every passing wind of doctrine, by the adroitness of men who are dexterous in devising error; we are to hold by the truth, and by our love to grow up wholly unto Him" (Eph. 4:13-14,M).

No current educational theory adequately accounts for this end-product of a sound program of Christian education. That children have grown up in the Church and come to a religion of maturity is an acknowledged fact, but it has never been the conscious aim of the educational system within the Churches as far as statements of purpose and method are concerned. Horace Bushnell's *Christian Nurture*, with its concern for the relationship between home and Church as the matrix of Christian nurture, came the closest to seeing this point of view, but those who used Bushnell's insights never adequately comprehended the organic connection between content and method, and they blurred the necessary relation between home and Church. Out of the tremendous concern for the present situation in Christian educational circles, Paul Vieth's *The Church and Christian Education* deals with all the factors involved, and Ernest Ligon's *A Greater Generation* is an important contribution to understanding the role of parents in the Church's program, but it has not been made clear how we can use the most effective of modern educational methods to teach a profoundly Christian theology in terms of the relationship between deeply held convictions and Christian behavior.

Those who are aware of the theological deficiencies in modern education have failed to see clearly the answer to the problem. The solution is not to inject theology into an otherwise non-theological approach to Christian education, for that is to get caught in the vicious circle of repeating the cycle of old mistakes. Theology, which is truth from a Christian perspective, must be the presupposition of any curriculum. There is a proper theological perspective for using the Bible, for examining the life of Christ, for approaching Christian history, for studying the meaning of worship and of the sacraments, for finding the Christian answer to individual behavior problems, for looking on the social situation, and for building Christian fellowship between the Churches.

For the Churches corporately to find an answer to such problems as these, means that the educators must become theologians, and the theologians must become educators, and the writers of lesson materials must be grounded thoroughly in both educational theory and theological method. Every aid must be sought from the findings of child and adult psychology, secular educational experience, and the sociology of learning, and in so far as the underlying theological pre--suppositions are sound, the Church's educational system may make use of the findings of all the sciences related to secular educational theory.

II

Other elements enter the picture as we examine the clue to Christian education. There are the practical problems of insufficient funds, inadequate time during the week for Christian education, untrained teachers in the Church schools, untrained and sometimes indifferent clergy, and improper equipment. These are difficult barriers to overcome even when the theory is sound, although it is not our purpose to deal with them in these chapters.

There are other elements in the theory of education which must be brought to bear on the present situation. The first of these is an understanding of the place of the home in the educational development of little Christians. It is a generally acknowledged fact that the little child gets his fundamental training in religious and character development before he is exposed to any kind of formal education in school or Church. The patterns of his reactions to all kinds of stimuli are built into habits during the early years. There is little chance that the Church in one hour or so per week (and against the background of a secular home and school) can do more than build on the habit patterns already established. Therefore, it is important that the significance of the relation between home and Church be realized within the elementary educational theory of the Church. The Christian home may be the greatest aid to the Church, and through their mutual interdependence there is the opportunity for a more sound and permanent Christian education.

Experiments along these lines are being carried out in many areas of the Church's life. There are experiments in the pre-school age-group, where parents are assisted by the Church in providing the conditions under which Christian growth may be furthered. So far, the Church has not been prepared to provide adequate guidance to parents, but the realizing of the need for this type of cooperation merits our hope that something significant may develop in terms of a new educational philosophy.

Cooperation between parents and the Church is really just beginning at the point where the child enters Church school, but often that is where they are cut off. Yet if there is to be any significant relationship between what is done at Church school and the child's daily life, the cooperation of parents is equally necessary at this point, and throughout the adolescent period as well. Some new lesson materials make a place for the parents in their methods, and in more advanced plans parents must actually take part in the Sunday schedule and then be ready to make reports on the progress of their children. While parents at the beginning of such an experiment are unprepared to give much help, by proper education they may become more effective than the average teacher. At this point, the educational theory is sound but it needs to be implemented as it is put into more widespread practice.

Because religion deals so much with intangibles, with subtly changing attitudes, and with the development and growth of the spirit, it is often hard to measure progress. Parents have been enlisted to assist in measuring the improved spiritual characteristics of their children, and teachers have been instructed in recognizing the changes which indicate successful teaching. In the past, too often the only measure of a child's religious growth has been in his ability to memorize or recite various selections of words, which as an end in itself might be a worthwhile exercise in memory but which has practically no effect on the child's relation to God. In reaction against content-centered teaching, we have quite rightly discarded the emphasis on memory work as a token in itself of Christian development, but we still have not discovered how to make the truths of the Christian Gospel relevant to everyday living in terms which can be observed. The intangibles have remained too intangible to be seen, and yet only as Christians learn to practice and bear witness to the Gospel can there be any significant growth in wisdom and in favor with God and man. Our clue to Christian education does not point to an easy answer to this question, but it poses the problem in different terms, in that it insists that Christian growth is a process of increased integration centered on the living God who is in our midst.

In modern society, the home usually finds that the basic implications of daily living are based upon a secular philosophy. The family exists in a society which is governed by the mechanics of industrialism and by the economics of the profit system, and it is against this cultural infiltration that the Christian home must work. It is not a problem of building a Christian home in a Christian society (and indeed the problem has never been that simple); it is rather the discovery of the relevance of the Christian home within a society which permits, condones, and approves many un-Christian motives and actions.

Our fundamental educational procedures in the public schools are based primarily upon the principles of a secular society. While it is true that Christianity provides the religious nucleus of American culture, it is also evident that the predominant educational philosophy of the United States is a pragmatic and instrumentalist approach which has little or no place for religion. The public schools, important and significant as they are in American culture, are hardly allies of the Christian Church and Christian home in the field of basic theological motives and assumptions. The school may well be an ally in terms of cooperative activities, and it may supplement the work of the Church and home without distorting what the Christian is trying to achieve, but there is an underlying difference of philosophy which must be recognized.

The child is exposed first of all to the influence of his parents, and this is where the crucial influence on character development takes place. At a certain point, the schools begin to have as much as or more influence than the parents, although the parents never cease to have an obligation in this regard. The Church is always on the sidelines, making use of whatever experiences the home and school and community provide for a Christian interpretation of life. This means that the Church should often sit in judgment on the child's experiences which run in opposition to the basic assumptions of a Christian society. At other times, the Church will find in these experiences rich and abiding meanings which are ways of opening the child's awareness of God.

The Church also provides a new set of experiences, which are the product of the Church's life of worship, study, fellowship, and service. These are small elements in the time span of the child, totaling at most only a little over an hour or two per week, but their significance far outweighs the brevity of the experiences. If conditions in the home and school are sufficiently related to what happens in Church, the Church becomes relevant as a basis for providing the deeper and richer meanings of life. But in many instances, the Church provides an isolated kind of experiences, where the child fails to see the relevance of what is happening, and thus he sees religion as divorced from life. This is due not only to a false concept of the Church's relation to society or to the inadequacy of educational method. The real failure is due to the inability to relate theology to life, and thus we are back to our original analysis that the weak link in modern Christian education is the failure to realize the proper place of the relevant truths of Christianity behind the child-centered and God-centered experiences of the learners. When theology is meaningful and related to life, it is possible to make use of the experiences of all of life to build a Christian perspective in the light of the learner's situation and age-group, illuminating those experiences with the peculiarly Christian experiences of worship, sacrament, preaching, study, fellowship, and work as found within the life of the Church.

III

The clue to Christian education is the rediscovery of a relevant theology which will bridge the gap between content and method, providing the background and perspective of Christian truth by which the best methods and content will be used as tools to bring the learners into the right relationship with the living God who is revealed to us in Jesus Christ, using the guidance of parents and the fellowship of life in the Church as the environment in which Christian nurture will take place.

I believe this clue rests in the picture of Jesus as a teacher or rabbi in the Gospels. He always assumed the basic truth of belief in God. He taught that God was our Father. He referred constantly to the fundamental truths revealed in the Old Testament. His theology was relevant to every situation in which he found himself. But he always taught in terms of a particular problem or of a specific individual or group. He related his theology to life. He spoke to the "growing edge" of his hearers, and he always led them beyond himself to a deeper loyalty to the Father. His parables were always "life situations to his hearers, and they saw the application of his teaching to their problems. He never watered down his theology, but he always made it speak to the situation. He did not speak or teach in abstractions.

So also, we are dealing with real children and real adults, and theology is simply "truth-about-God-in-relation-to-man." As adults, we should have mature beliefs, but we should teach these beliefs in terms of the experiences and capacities of the children and older learners, leading them always from their "growing edge" to the deeper meanings and appreciations of life. The chief source of all our teaching is the Bible, the chief interest of our teaching is the learners, and the chief end of our teaching is the God and Father of Jesus Christ.

Because Christianity is primarily an historical rather than a metaphysical religion, the center of the approach to God will be through Jesus Christ, and Jesus will always be seen against the historical background of the Incarnation. While one would not tell a kindergarten child that the Christmas story tells of the birth of the "incarnate Lord" and expect him to understand the phraseology, it would be necessary for the teacher and the writer of the lesson material to know this and to teach so that the child would not learn something foreign to this belief. Some educators might even decide that it would be better not to emphasize the "baby Jesus" at the expense of later Christian faith, for sometimes a child fails to get beyond thinking of Jesus as a baby. In other words, method and content would be judged both by mature theological considerations and by sound knowledge of how the child's personality reacts.

We have acquired a great deal of information concerning the behavior and thoughts of the little child, we have experimented widely and wisely with the learning process at all age-levels, and we have made great use of these new insights, but we have never brought theology to bear upon them. Theology has been taught in opposition to child psychology, and this has been done at the expense of both theology and the child. The new task is to make theology relevant, realizing that the goal of Christian education is Christian truth, that truth may be acquired only through the interpretation of experience, and that we become Christians only as we use truth to place ourselves in commitment to the living God revealed to us in Jesus Christ and through the fellowship of the Church.

To make this specific, it is our intention in the succeeding chapters to take the basic theological presuppositions of a Christian educational philosophy, and to illustrate how the clue described in this chapter may be used in actual situations to realize the objectives of a theologically sound Christian education.

* * * * * * * * * *

Lewis Joseph Sherrill
(1959)

[From *The Gift of Power* (New York: The Macmillan Company, 1955),
pp. 44-58.]

RELATIONSHIPS IN COMMUNITY

The term "community" implies that persons sustain some
kind of relationship with one another. When persons are
brought into association with one another, relationships are
set up between them.   The relationships may be felt as
closeness, or as distance.   In any case when persons are
brought to bear upon one another relationships of some kind
start up between them.

A "relationship" in its simplest form is that which exists
between two entities and affects them both, when they are
brought to bear upon each other. This "betweenness" is a
dynamic field in which each entity "does something to" the
other, such as attracting, staying neutral, or repelling.

If this is put in terms of human relationships, when two
persons are brought to bear upon each other they "do
something to" each other, whether it is building each other
up, or tearing each other down, or whatever else. What they
do to each other is a function of the relationship that exists
between them; that is, it depends upon the nature of the
relationship between them.   The process of affecting each
other in relationships is interaction between persons.

If we take more complex cases where several persons are
in interaction, the same principles hold.   For relationships
may exist among several persons, as in a family or in any
other group.   Here also persons are interacting in
relationships and in doing so are affecting one another. This
too is a dynamic field, but an extremely complicated one. It

is an intricate network of crisscrossing relationships, such as the relationship of each person to every other person, person to person through a third person, person to group, and group to person.

Moreover the field of interrelatedness and interaction is highly sensitive, being subject to sudden shifts of feeling. For example, a group may at one time engage itself in building up one of its members, but at another time may turn upon him and begin savagely to "take him to pieces." But here, as in the simpler case of the one-to-one relationship, what happens within the persons involved depends upon the nature of the relationships between them; the process of its happening is interaction between persons.

Relationships and interaction are of the highest importance for two reasons among many. The first of these is that they appear to determine the character structure of the individual self. We have in view here a generalization which seems to be justified by the findings in many branches of psychological study, and which seems also to be borne out by studies of the past. It is this. The self is formed in its relationships with others. If it becomes de-formed, it becomes so in its relationships. If it is re-formed or trans-formed, that too will be in its relationships.

The expression "in a relationship" as here used means not only within it, but in virtue of the interaction between selves which takes place. In any such statement we must allow, of course, for congenital deficiencies of mind or body, and for inroads upon the body by diseases which impair the physical organism. But we are thinking now of the self which one becomes, whatever his endowment. This becoming, it appears, is a becoming in and by virtue of relationships, according as one's native endowment and native potentialities will allow.

The other reason for the high importance of relationships and interaction is the reverse of what has just been said. It may be expressed in this summary but simple way: a community is a body of relationships which affect the becoming of its individual members. A community "does something to" the people who compose it, and they in turn do something to it, as the people of the community interact with one another.

The relationships which carry the greatest power to affect the character structure of the young self are those that exist within that most intimate of all forms of community, the family. In our culture ordinarily the earliest years are spent in the midst of whatever relationships the young self sustains with the mother or the mother substitute, the father or the father substitute, the siblings, if any, and whoever else makes up the household. In the case of those who do not grow up in a household, the same point still holds; namely, that one grows up in the midst of a body of relationships.

It appears further that in those early years the character structure begins to take shape long before the child is able to talk. Indeed, there is much evidence to support the view that the character structure begins to take its form from the day of birth, of course within the limits of one's native endowment and potentialities.

The relationships in which the young grow up seem always in actual life to contain some kind of mingling of creative and destructive interaction. Of course, these relationships may be, and very often are, of the highest possible order. In that event they tend to affirm the selfhood of the young, and to lead toward the realization of the potential self. But they may, and it would seem that they commonly do, also contain some element of greater or lesser strength which threatens the full realization of the potential self. With this basic character structure, whether for better or for worse, the very young begin to move out little by little from the circle of the family.

As the younger person begins to move out from the smaller orbit of the family into a larger orbit, he is seeking some kind of relationship and some kind of interaction which the members of his family cannot supply. In doing so he encounters others who are in a generally similar situation. These all are seeking community, whether in play groups or clique or club or gang. The resulting tightly knit togetherness of the young with their own kind in some form of community is a notable feature of the transition from the relatively safe community of the family to the psychologically hazardous situation of those who are just coming into physical maturity.

In maturity the search for community commonly continues as people seek to associate themselves with others in some form of togetherness. Nor does the search for community cease with the passing of the decades. To the end of life there is the need to be bound up together in some manner with others of our kind. This is the more important as aging comes, whether for those who have known profoundly satisfying family life, only to find it breaking up around them; or for those who have now known it and now feel that the coming of the last years carries the threat of devastating loneliness at the end.

The need for community is not respecter of social and eco-nomic levels. But finding it is another matter. The poor, needing community, often can find it only in the fact of their poverty. The desperate need it, but often can find common ground only in the feeling that every man's hand is against them. The comfortably well off perhaps find it easier than any others to attain community with their kind. The very wealthy and their children perhaps find it harder than any others to attain deep community, being shut out from so much of the common lot of men, and exposed to so many persons who cultivate acquaintance with some concealed motive.

All these, the young, the desperate, the poor, and the wealthy, different though they are in so many other ways, have this in common: they live under the threat of being excluded from the deepest community so that they are pushed into partial community or into separateness. They share also a healthy suspicion of being "taken in" by any kind of community which will try to exploit them.

Hence the deeper need for community is a need for a kind of community in which the bond of association is some concern which is held in common. No concern they share in common is any more profound than the desire to find oneself and be a person in one's own right, regardless of age or status, regardless of poverty or wealth.

Beyond all this it is being borne home to us now that the right to be man which the small communities of men attempt to guarantee to their members is under threat from the schism between sovereign national states, and especially from the great schism between the West and the East. These forms of schism make up the great splitness in the world as a whole which now holds the fear of destruction before all men's eyes.

In the face of this threat there seems to be a great ground of swell of longing for "one world" in which not only nations but individual men live under law to which all are subject, not under fear. To attain this is a political task. But how is this to be attained apart from a reconciliation between men so deeply rooted in the spirits of men that the common will to peace will brook no more delay? This is a spiritual task.

Community, then, as we are considering it here, has a threefold aspect. People seek community with others not only for the sake of togetherness as such, but for the sake also of supplying-deficiencies in the relationships they have already known. In such community as they find, they affect and are affected by others in interaction with them. And the interaction commonly contains the two elements so often called to attention; namely, both potentially constructive, and potentially destructive, forces.

Thus the community which one finds may, on the one hand, provide the opportunity for creative interaction in relationships which may reduce or even remove some of the threats which one feels, so enhancing selfhood. In this way some of the deficiencies in the existing self may be supplied, or an already healthy character structure may be further supported and strengthened. But on the other hand the community which one finds may involve him in the kind of interaction which reinforces the threats that he already feels, or may even produce new ones to which he has been a stranger until now. In this event the community which he finds tends to undermine a character structure which was already weak, and may begin to tear down one which was healthy.

Persons, of course, seek many kinds of community. Perhaps no one kind of community can supply all the legitimate needs for community which any one person feels. It is not our purpose to consider, or even attempt to name, them all. Instead, we turn now more specifically to the Christian community.

THE NATURE OF THE CHRISTIAN COMMUNITY

When we ask about the nature of the Christian community we must, of course, ask about the nature of the Christian church. The term "the Christian community" is but one name among many for the Christian church, bringing out one of its aspects. But the moment we begin to inquire into the nature of the church we are met by a surprising fact which George Florovsky, among many, has called to attention. He writes, "It is impossible to start with a formal definition of the church. For strictly speaking there is none which can claim any doctrinal authority."

He goes on to say that no definition is to be found in the Fathers, nor in the schoolmen, not even in St. Thomas Aquinas. None was given by the Ecumenical Councils, and none by the Great Councils, including those of Trent and the Vatican. He continues, quoting from Bartmann, "The church existed for about fifteen hundred years without reflecting upon its nature and without attempting its clarification by a logical conception." And he adds:

In our time, it seems, one has to get beyond the modern theological disputes to regain a wider historical perspective, to recover the true "catholic mind," which would embrace the whole of the historical experience of the church in its pilgrimage through the ages. One has to return from the schoolroom to the worshiping church and perhaps to change the school-dialect of theology for the pictorial nd metaphorical language of Scripture. The very nature of the church can be rather depicted and described than properly defined. And surely this can be done only from within the church. Probably even this description will be convincing only for those of the church. The Mystery is apprehended only by faith.

We have referred to Florovsky's statement at this length for two reasons. The first is that the church's experience through a span of many centuries is comparable with that of a healthy-minded individual, in that it had the strong self-consciousness of being a church; and as long as it wa sure of itself it experienced itself as a unique entity without needing to stop and consciously define itself. The second reason is that the church, again like the individual, has to be experienced from within in order to be known. And as Florovsky suggests, this knowing of itself from within consists primarily in knowing itself as a worshiping community.

Our task, then, is to try to identify and briefly state some of the principal ways in which a Christian community experiences itself and knows itself as a worshiping community.

In the first place, the Christian community is a self-transcending community and knows itself as such, however the matter may be expressed from one communion to another. In saying this we are not forgetting the fact that a particular Christian community, a "local church," is embedded in the social order. It is set down in a particular locality. It owns property. It is subject to, and is protected by, civil law. It has some kind of stake, large or small, in the status quo. It is sensitive to cultural conditions, for its people are people of a particular time and place. A great deal more could be said in recognition of the church's inextricable involvement in the world as it is.

Nevertheless as a Christian community it transcends all this even while remaining in it. For so soon as it begins to act corporately it orients itself to another dimension and knows itself to be rooted and grounded in that other dimension. The nature of that other dimension is indicated at once, for example, by the very word for community which it uses. That word is *koinonia*, which means fellowship, communion, sharing, participating in, the state of being in communication; in short, *koinonia is* community.

But *koinonia* is a kind of community which transcends ordinary human community in that God is present and participant in the community. For the connotation of koinonia is that the Spirit of God is forthgoing into, and present in, every relationship within the community. Thus it signifies that every relationship in the Christian community participates in God and God in it, whether it be the relationship of person to person, or of each to all, or all to each; while the whole community as a whole participates in God and God in it. Thus koinonia is by its nature a community intimately indwelt by the Spirit.

The orientation of the Christian community to God from whom it has its being is of course symbolized in many ways. For example, the Long Meter Doxology, used in many congregations at the opening of the service of worship, voices it in the familiar words:

> Praise God, from whom all blessings flow;
> Praise him, all creatures here below;
> Praise him above, ye heavenly host;
> Praise Father, Son, and Holy Ghost.

And the equally familiar Apostolic Benediction with which the assemblage is often dismissed, contains the word koinonia: "The grace of the Lord Jesus Christ, and the love of God, and the communion of the Holy Spirit be with you all"; which is saying, at the very end of the moments spent together in worship, "Let this communion go out with you unbroken into whatever is before you."

The idea of a community which transcends itself is wrapped up in many of the familiar words for the church. Indeed, the word "church" itself does this; for an ecclesia, or church, is an assemblage of those who have been "called out," and "the church of God" is those who have been called out from the world by God, to meet God. Again, it is "the Body of Christ," to denote a prolonging of that Self in bodily form to the end of time.

In Scripture it is called by many names which indicate its self-transcendent nature. It is "the house of God," "the household of God," "the household of faith," where the idea of the church as a family, men as brothers, and God as Father, is prominent. There are terms which express the idea of a living organism, like a body or a plant, having Jesus Christ as the head of the body or the trunk of the plant. There are terms that express the idea of the believer's body as a temple of the Spirit, and the community as a living temple built out of living stones; and numerous others. In all of them the suggestion of the community's organic togetherness with that togetherness indwelt by God is strong.

The self-transcendence of the Christian community is affirmed in the act of worship itself. In worship men turn beyond themselves and affirm God. This is true, for example, in prayer in such acts as adoration, thanksgiving, confession, supplication for oneself, and intercession for others.

Self-transcendence is affirmed by the sacraments. There we are confronted by the body and blood of Jesus Christ during the sacrament of holy communion, and we are confronted by the spirit of God during the sacrament of baptism. Similarly during such other sacraments as a particular community may celebrate, men are confront~d by some aspect of the grace of God.

The Christian community's self-transcendence is affirmed by the reading and hearing of the "Word of God which is contained in the Scriptures of the Old and New Testaments," and by the careful teaching of it, whether from the pulpit, or in small face-to-face groups. The reading of Scripture in public worship originated as an act of teaching both in Jewish synagogue worship and in the Christian service. The teaching was in this instance first of all a confronting of the community by the Word of God. Thus it is of the genius of both the Jewish and the Christian community to embed teaching in the corporate worship of the community.

The self-transcendence of the Christian community is affirmed again by singing. Even the so-called subjective hymns, self-searching as they are, affirm that one searches himself in the Presence. But more yet the great "objective" hymns of the church affirm God in adoration, thanksgiving, joy. And the great music of the church affirms it, especially when virtuosity and self-display are put behind the back while instruments and voices make one great harmony from uplifted hearts.

Once more, the self-transcendence of the particular Christian community is affirmed whenever that community links itself in any manner, by thought or action, with the wider community, the holy catholic or universal church. The evidences of the self-transcendent nature of the Christian community might be adduced at still greater length. But the sum of the matter as far as self-transcendence is concerned may be expressed in this way: The Christian community by virtue of its own nature is in the unique position of being a true community of living persons, but of being able also at the same time to stand above itself and view itself under the light of revelation and eternity.

As a little band of men, women, and children they know and affirm that they participate in that innumerable company of persons in all times and places who, in being found by God who is altogether worthy of supreme devotion, have begun to find themselves. And they are never more truly themselves than when they affirm him in the triumphant hallelujahs of Christian faith.

In the second place this scene of a community which transcends itself in a koinonia with God is precisely the scene into which men come bearing the intimate personal concerns of daily life. As has so often been pointed out, it is only after we have first made the affirmation of God by praying,

> Our Father who art in heaven, hallowed by
> 　　thy name.
> Thy kingdom come.
> They will be done in earth as it is in heaven,
> 　　that we are ready in spirit to pray,
> Give us this day our daily bread.
> And forgive us our debts, as we forgive our
> 　　debtors.
> And lead us not into temptation, but deliver us
> 　　from evil.

Having so prayed, the community in its corporate prayer can then again affirm its transcendent dimension:

> For thine is the kingdom, and the power, and
> 　　the glory, forever. Amen.

For the Christian community, which is a self-transcendent community, is at the same time a community of the concerned. And what are the concerns it carried within itself? Exactly those of which we have spoken in the first two chapters; these or any others which go down to the roots of man's finite existence, or any such as spring up out of them.

If we are members of a family we come, or we may come, as a family group. This may be literally and physically true, as when we sit together. But in a larger sense it may always be true, matter what has happened physically to the family group. Spiritually no one ever enters the sanctuary alone. He is always surrounded and accompanied by all whom he has ever loved, whether they are still counted among the living or have joined the greater assembly of the undying.

Into the worshiping community we come in our anxiety. We come, it may well be, frankly and unashamedly concerned over our own inward situation. It is our right to come in this concern, for who is to say that this was not the first reason we were called out to come? We come, too, equally and it may be much more concerned over those with whom our lives are knit together. There are great spiritual utterances in which a man prays to God that if any of his beloved people are to be blotted out, he may be blotted out with them.

We come concerned to know whether there is hope; not hope in the abstract, but hope for us, hope for me, hope for our time and for our world. It is to this concern to know whether there is hope, that the Christian gospel is addressed.

We come concerned over our relationships--to God, to other men, to oneself. To this concern, to say it again, the gospel is a proclamation of hope. The gospel is the affirmation, proclaimed as good news, that even as Jesus Christ died and rose again from the dead, so may we be raised up, now in the present hour, from our deadness to walk in newness of life.

Further, we come knowing well enough that in coming we shall be challenged as to our own responsibility as a community and as individuals. We have many forms of concern about this responsibility; as, for example, an apprehensiveness that others will press upon us a concern which we cannot feel; or an apprehensiveness that the concern which others feel will not match our own in intensity; or perhaps an apprehensiveness because we feel no concern, or because we feel our own concern too deeply as if one finite creature were taking upon himself all the burdens of the world.

A sense of corporate responsibility commonly characterizes the Christian community. This may be a sense of responsibility for the living or the well-being of its own members. It may be a sense of responsibility for reaching out in any of many ways beyond itself, notably in evangelistic and missionary effort, and in specific tasks or amelioration and reform. Thus whenever human selfhood is encroached upon, threatened, undermined, men commonly sense with sure intuition that this is a concern of the Christian community, or is due to be. They may fight back savagely at the church if they feel that it is encroaching upon them with its claims for human justice. Yet they know that if the church feels no concern it is not only a traitor to the society in which it exists, but a traitor to itself.

The fact that this sense of corporate responsibility tends to exist in some form and to some degree wherever the church exists partly accounts for the further accompanying fact that the church is a sort of embodied conscience within the social body. As such it stands as a threat to many. Some of these are persons who have had to free themselves from a morbid conscience based on some kind of idealized image. They believe -that --religion as they knew it contributed- to -- morbidity, and they wish no more of it.

Wherever this feeling is well founded, such persons stand as a living reproach to any Christian community which, in offering salvation, succeeded only in putting men into a bondage which they could escape only by escaping the church. Some, however, to whom the church stands as a threat in the conscience are persons to whom any reminder of man's spiritual nature is an unwelcome reminder of a presently unspiritual existence which they have no desire to forsake.

At its best, in exercising its great function of moral reminder the church stands in the midst of the City of Man and calls upon it to become the City of God. At its best, too, this is no crying out of "holier than thou." For living in the midst of a disordered society in which it participates, it transcends itself by its prophetic word to itself and to the people of its day, speaking forth concerning men's sin and calling for repentance.

In the third place, not only does the Christian community transcend itself and bring its own profoundest concerns in to the place of meeting with God; it also knows that there is splitness within itself. Its people know there are rifts in the church, very deep rifts which neither the grace of God nor the passing of time has healed. Its people, knowing this, know that wholeness is not yet in the church itself.

This splitness exists between branch and branch of the church; it exists between the particular Christian community and its neighboring Christian community, and sometimes within a particular community which is divided into factions. It often exists within one denomination, as when such a body is rent by controversy.

Splitness has led, of course, to every conceivable kind of conflict: to wars of religion, to inquisitions of many sorts in which Christians persecute Christians, and to the laying of rival religious claims before the civil courts for adjudication. And it has divided the church into denominations competing with one another for members, for territory, for privilege, for prestige, and for power.

The people of the churches are intensely aware of the riots which divide the Christian church. Some regard it with incredulity and shame. Some hold to the division in a state of mingled conviction and regret. But some make their own persisting in division a matter of pride, because of what one's own branch of the church has meant in history. All these are ambivalent feelings, in which the possibility of repentance and reconciliation lies near the surface.

But there are those in whom this form of repentance seems impossible. Assured that they participate in the only true church, they assign places of spiritual peril to all outside it. And all this, being observed by the people who are outside the church, is understood clearly by them to be scandal, a stumblingblock.

Yet this is by no means all there is to say about the splitness of the church. For within the present century a prolonged and remarkable ecumenical movement has been under way, representing the effort from within the church to heal these divisions. This movement has expressed itself in a long series of unions between large denominations in Canada; and in the United States where the fragmenting of the church has proceeded to an extreme degree. Similar unions have taken place in many other lands.

The ecumenical movement is not merely on a national scale, but on one that is worldwide. The story is far too long to recount here, but for instance the Oxford and Edinburgh conferences of 1937, and the meeting of the World Council of Churches at Amsterdam in 1948, stand as monuments of spiritual yearning and striving on both sides of the Second World War.

So also in the United States the formation in 1908 of the Federal Council of the Churches of Christ in America, and of its successor the National Council of Churches, represent the springing up of the federal principle in lieu of deeper unity, before and after participation in world conflict. Many see in the ecumenical movement an inflow of the Spirit into the church at the very time when the demonic passion for destruction threatens to mount to proportions of global suicide.

Nevertheless one cannot study the church in history nor experience it as a living community in the present without having to admit that the existing church carries within itself powers both of a spiritual and of a demonic kind. It carries spiritual power which makes for the redemption and wholeness of the human self, of the church, and of society. but it also carries demonic power because men as human creatures carry potentially demonic power within themselves, and it is human creatures who make up the Christian community.

If any should flinch from the term "demonic to denote any element or power within man, we ask only that he look at the toll of death and destruction wrought by man upon man in the present century and find for himself a more fitting term to denote the driving force of the passions let loose. Men with the capacity for this destructive power can unleash it in the name of God just as they can in the name of the state. Is it too much to say that there is that within a man which often secretly longs for a God who will command him to destroy?

But always in facing the demonic and destructive element which is so intertwined with the spiritual redemptive, we are brought back to the fact that the Christian community is a worshiping community. When we say that, we are also saying that in deliberately coming to meet with God man is coming to be met by God. There into the meeting place we come in anxiety and come also, it may be, to place our claims upon God and enlist him, as it were, to sit beside us to furnish the power and pay the tolls as we drive the car of our own destiny. But there in that same meeting place we are met by One who confronts us with his claims upon us and our living. We come asking from out of the framework of one dimension which is within us. But we are spoken to in the framework of another dimension which is also within us. Our responses make up the destiny which we choose.

But this is the story of revelation and encounter, into which we are to inquire more closely in later chapters. Here it must be enough to say that when the human self, whatever its brokenness and sin, comes to the place of meeting it is to be met by another Self who is within and yet beyond the human self. And in affirming God within that encounter, man is not only affirming Another. He is also affirming his life, but it is his eternal life which he is affirming. And he is affirming that it is not merely his duty, but rather his right, to live now in that dimension.

* * * * * * * * * *

D. Campbell Wyckoff
(1959)

[From *The Gospel and Christian Education* (Philadelphia: The Westminster Press, 1959), pp. 97-112.]

At the same time that it is the responsibility of Christian education to be the church's effective servant, it is also up to it to be in a position to know and to contest the inroads of the cultural situation at the necessary points. To do this, it needs a theory that is adequate, both theologically and educationally. That theory, in order to be useful, has to be expressed in terms that can be readily understood and grasped by everyone involved in Christian education, including the layman and the learner.

In order to be readily communicable, the whole theory may well be informed by a guiding principle that is at once adequate, simple, and clear. This guiding principle can give Christian education sure direction by infusing its objectives, its curriculum principles, and its principles of administration. It will also focus the various elements that make up Christian education (all the concerns of the Christian faith and the Christian life), so that their meaning and use will be unmistakably clear.

It has been variously suggested that elements like the Bible, Christian doctrine, problem-solving, "life," experience, the child, the person, the church, and the person of Christ might serve as the basis for such a guiding principle.

The element that seems, however, to hold most promise of being able to focus the other elements, to give unmistakable guidance to Christian education, and at the same time to be adequate both from a theological and an educational point of view, is the gospel.

It appears, then, that the most promising clue to orienting Christian education theory so that it will be both worthy and communicable is to be found in recognizing and using the gospel of God's redeeming activity in Jesus Christ as its guiding principle.

The suggestion that the gospel be used as the basic guide for Christian education theory is supported by give arguments:

1.   Revelation--the Word of God--is central in Christian education theory.

2.   The gospel--God's redeeming activity in Jesus Christ--is the very heart and point of the Word he has spoken to men in their self-centered helplessness throughout the ages, and the very heart and point of the Word he speaks to men today.

3.   The gospel is the clue to the meaning of history.

4.   The gospel is the clue to the meaning of existence.

5.   The gospel is the reason for the church's existence: it brings the church into existence; it sustains the church; it informs, directs, and corrects the church.

After discussing each of these points, we will be in a position to see whether the gospel can be properly used as the basis for a guiding principle.

1. *The Word of God*

In *The Task of Christian Education* (Chapter 6), after pointing out that in ordinary speech a word is a way of getting something across so that it will be understood, I discussed the Word of God as God's way of getting himself, in the most complete sense, across to men:

"The Word of God is God's attempt to get the nature of his being and his will across to us so that we shall understand it. Of course, it is more than the spoken word. As a rule, we regard the Word of God as not so much spoken as written, written in a book. But this again is not by any means the whole concept of the Word. Look again at ordinary words and you see what is involved. To help people to understand something you can show them what it is; you can tell them what it is; and you can make it possible for them constantly to be reminded of it. God uses all these methods: demonstrating, telling, and reminding us of his nature, existence, and truth. He shows us what he is like; here is the Word made flesh, Jesus Christ, pre-existent, existent in history, and eternally existent as the living Christ, the living Lord. He leaves us a written record of what he is like; here is the Bible, the Word in written form. Furthermore, he continually illumines our understanding of what he is like; here is the testimony of the Spirit to the Word within our hearts."

The Word of God is revelation. It is God's disclosure of himself, his revelation of himself.

In a deep sense the Word of God is spoken to us; God discloses himself to us. We have the opportunity and the responsibility to listen, to understand, to answer, and to become and do what is clearly implied. This is a dynamic encounter, by the very nature of the Word not so much an encounter with an idea or proposition as an encounter of a person-to-person kind.

Because we are rational beings, and always try to think out the meaning of our experience by translating it into ideas, we respond to the Word of God by trying to explain to ourselves and to other people what the encounter means to us. This gives rise to theology and doctrine, the formulation of the Christian faith. Let us come directly to the point--What is the Christian faith? What is our interpretation of our encounter with the Word of God?

The Christian faith has a source; its doctrine of God speaks to this matter. It deals with a problem; its doctrines of man and sin explain what this problem is. It believes that the problem has been solved; the doctrines of the covenant, the incarnation, the atonement, and the living Word attempt to explain how God has dealt with and solved the human problem. It believes that God has entrusted his work in the world to his people, and that he guides them by his Spirit; here it develops its doctrine of the church, including the church's ministry of the Word and sacraments and the church's mission. Christian faith has a goal; its belief about its goal is the subject of its doctrine of the fulfillment of personal destiny and human history. God's revelation of the meaning of life and history is thus the source and subject of the Christian faith.

It has been amply demonstrated that such an understanding of the Christian faith is absolutely indispensable to a theory of Christian education that is theologically worthy. Any Christian education theory that did not make this central would be distorted and would lack permanent value. Revelation, and the Christian faith as the witness to revelation, are thus central to Christian education theory.

The purpose of Christian education has often been glibly and superficially described as "to teach people about God." In a deep sense, this is the purpose of Christian education. And if it is, then the Word of God--his telling us who he really is--is the very heart of it. And the theological witness to the Word is of major importance in enabling men to listen to the Word, understand, answer, and become and do what is demanded.

2. *The Gospel--the Heart of the Word*

To a person or to a world so wrapped up in itself that it has never considered such a possibility, the fact of God's having revealed himself, the fact that in so doing he has revealed the meaning of life and history, the fact that he has made the human problem clear and has solved it, comes--if it does not seem like utter foolishness--as news, good news, the good news.

The New Testament writers saw in Jesus Christ the climax and fulfillment of the whole drama of history and revelation. The fact of who he was and what he did was the best news that man had ever received, or could ever receive. Such phrases as "the Word made flesh" and "the living Word" are a sort of symbolic shorthand by which~the tremendous significance of the gospel is indicated.

The definition of the term "gospel" in the concordance of *The Westminster Study Edition of The Holy Bible* (The Westminster Press, 1948) is this: "The word means 'good news,' 'glad tidings.' Hence it is used of the message

proclaimed by Jesus himself concerning the coming Kingdom
of God, and then of the story of God's redeeming activity
through the life, death, and resurrection of Jesus Christ,
proclaimed by the apostles and recorded by the Evangelists."

The gospel is the Bible's essential unity, since it is the
gospel that the Old Testament anticipates, and since it is the
gospel that constitutes the message of the New Testament.
At its climax, according to Millar Burrows (in *An Outline of
Biblical Theology*, The Westminster Press, 1946), the Old
Testament proclaims the expectation of the gospel:

"Failure to do God's will as he has revealed it incurs
judgment; but God does not leave the guilty without hope: he
offers the undeserving sinner redemption and reveals the way
to obtain it.   The promise of the new covenant includes
forgiveness.   This note sounds strongly in the later prophets,
especially Second Isaiah, who again and again proclaims the
good news of deliverance.   This is the origin of the Christian
word "gospel."   The law shows what God requires and the
penalties of disobedience; the gospel shows the way of
deliverance when man has failed to meet the requirements.
This is what Paul means by justification, God's free gift to the
sinner."

The gospel constitutes the message of the New Testament.
In his analysis of the word "gospel" (in *A Theological Word
Book of the Bible*, p. 100; The Macmillan Company, 1950),
Alan Richardson says:

"After the death and resurrection of Jesus the content of
the gospel, as it is understood by the apostolic church, is
Christ himself.   It is no longer simply 'the gospel of the
Kingdom of God' (though, of course, that is involved), but is
'the gospel of Jesus Christ, the Son of God'--a phrase in
which every word must be given its full significance.   It is 'the
gospel of God,' the saving message which God has addressed
to the world, first by way of anticipation in the Scriptures,
and now finally in the living Word, Jesus Christ.   It is
therefore supremely the message of the cross and the

resurrection, and it is 'the power of God unto salvation to every one that believeth.' The church itself is built upon this one gospel and is indeed a fellowship in the gospel. The gospel must always be received personally by faith. For those who thus receive it the gospel is always 'news,' breaking in freshly upon them and convincing them afresh, though they may first have heard it and accepted it long ago." (Used by permission.)

It was in the mid-1930's that, browsing in a bookstore on upper Amsterdam Avenue in New York, I came across Principal Alex. Martin's *The Finality of Jesus for Faith* (T. & T. Clark, Edinburgh). The book had been written in 1933. It was a period when the churches were given to "religiousness," or to a combination of literalistic pedantry and sentimental emotionalism. Into such an atmosphere Principal Martin's direct witness to the gospel came with intense clarity. It has been my polestar ever since. He points to the gospel as "the supreme service rendered to men by Jesus." That service, he says, does not consist:

"...in instruction alone; and it is only less inadequate to put Him forward as exhibiting a pattern to be reproduced. He does more even than introduce a new ethico-religious type into history. What he assumes to do is different in kind from this. The word for it is 'reconciliation.'... He redeems from the most intimate and grievous of all the contradictions of the human lot, the distress and slavery of sin. Through him, and above all through his death, his followers find harmony with the world, restoration to fellowship with the Power at the heart of it; and with that is given the assurance of victory and peace. It is a matter of experience that morally distracted souls do thus find the readjustment with Reality which they crave. They do, in plain spiritual fact, pass into "the Holiest of all"--to the very heart of Existence where alone spiritual nature can rest--through the rent veil of this Man's flesh. They consciously draw nearer very God the more they become one with the dying Jesus, entering more deeply into his consciousness of the hateful thing that brought him to his end, acknowledging with him submissively the righteousness of the divine reaction against it, and taking hold with him believingly of the mercy--discovered in the cry, 'Father, forgive them, for they know not what they do'--that nevertheless is over all.

"To express it otherwise: theological terms and Biblical figures and modes of speech apart, what is it, in bare spiritual simplicity, that Jesus has achieved for men?... In the case of a sinless nature it might perhaps be [possible to have] a free spiritual fellowship with the living God in trustful obedience and love [without Jesus]: in the nature we know, darkened, degraded, distraught through evil.. the fulfillment of the divine purpose in our life is hindered fatally. Only Jesus helps men here, and above all in his dying.   As they identify themselves with that dread experience, believing men find themselves reunited with the spiritual order they belong to; the will is restored to freedom which had willfully become unfree; and deliverance is experienced from the impotence and disability of every kind which had followed on that. Since, in and through the dying Jesus, they come into contact with That in which he lived and moved and to whose care he at the last committed himself, and find it to be a living Power of Love bent on reversing the course of natural consequence, forgiving sin, and eliminating its power from life." (Used by permission.)

Thus the gospel--God's redeeming activity in Jesus Christ-- is the very heart and point of the Word he has spoken to men in their helplessness throughout the ages, and the very heart and point of the Word he speaks to men today.

3. *The Meaning of History*

The gospel is the clue to the meaning of history. God deals with man through the medium of history. The perception of history and historical relationships is man's God-given way of finding himself and the meaning of his life in the continuum of time.

Meaningful history is, looked at from a thoroughly realistic perspective, the account of God's relationships with man. History past is the story of what he has done with, for, and through man. History present is his current activities with, for, and through man. History future is what he intends to do with, for, and through man.

Suddenly, then, the Bible, with the gospel as its major motif, comes into perspective as "holy history." In this context it is clear that through his relations with the Hebrew people God indicated his redemptive purpose in history. Through the birth, life, death, resurrection, and ascension of his Son in history, he has established his redemptive purpose in history beyond the shadow of a doubt. In the same events he has guaranteed the victorious conclusion of his historical activity.

When the redemptive activity of God makes itself known to a man or a people it comes as the good news. Thus the gospel of Jesus Christ is God's revelation of the meaning of man's historical life.

Cultures rise, flourish, and decline in history. Their achievements and their conflicts are historical. In each culture, whatever its achievements or conflicts may be, the church is God's historical instrument, with a message to deliver. It is the gospel that constitute the message that the church has to deliver to each historical culture, else how can the culture know the meaning of the history of which it is a part?

4. *The Meaning of Existence*

But look at the matter, not from the perspective of the long sweep of God's purpose in history, which may seen very remote and impersonal, but from the perspective of the individual life, one's personal existence.

God's redemptive purpose seems to me to be very far removed unless I am involved in it. My immediate existence consists so largely of the world of my private thoughts and feelings that I tend to perceive my surroundings in terms of the patterns into which I have channeled by subjective needs.

I do see what is around, but unwittingly I see it the way I want to see it, the way I am habituated to see it.

Yet I want to live, and to live fully. As I try to do so, I seem to be prevented from it. The great desire of my heart, the thing that will make my life complete, is within my grasp. But even as I reach out for it, it eludes me. Or, if I do succeed in grasping it, it turns out to be not what I thought it would be, and is hardly worth the having.

I realize that what prevents me from living fully is that I see everything essentially from only one vantage point, and that from within. The world turns out to be not what it seems because my apprehension of it is completely distorted by my own desires, my preconceptions, my habits--in a word, by my whole point of view.

Someone tells me that what prevents me from living fully is my sin. Not so much the wrong things I do--they are more results than causes--but a whole warped attitude toward life. The universe as I see it revolves around me. I need to get outside myself, to gain perspective, to see things in true proportions and relationships.

Then the enormity of the situation dawns on me. It is arrogantly presumptuous of me to look at life as I do from my human, personal, egocentric point of view. I have simply been ignoring God. I have dethroned him from my life. My sin is thus radical sin, and deserving of death. This deserved penalty I would have to pay for having ignored and dethroned my God.

At the depth of my predicament I hear of the incarnation and the atonement (or I hear of the manger, the teacher, the healer, the cross, and the empty tomb). Then the overwhelming point of a sentence that perhaps had become obscure because of my having used it too much or too early speaks to me--"God so loved the world that he gave his only Son, that whoever believes in him should...have eternal life."

And as I respond, the old I does die, and He gives me a new birth of life in him.

This is the good news. Thus the gospel of Jesus Christ is God's revelation and living achievement of the meaning of existence, even of individual, personal existence.

5. *The Gospel and the Church*

In discussing the church and its educational work, I said that the church is the human instrumentality brought into being by God in Christ to continue his ministry of redemption to the world. Plainly, the gospel was and is the soul of that ministry.

The gospel is the reason for the church's existence. The reality of the gospel, its power, and the imperative for its communication brought the church into being. The gospel sustains the church in performing its functions (as outlined in Chapter 7 of *The Task of Christian Education*) in every generation and in every culture. The gospel, as the church's essential message, informs, directs, and corrects the church.

Thus, in a situation where the church and the culture are in tension (as they always are to some degree), it is the church's business to communicate the gospel. The gospel is what the church says to the culture. The church knows something that the culture does not know but needs to know. It is the work of the church to employ every means to deliver that urgently needed message.

The church's own members live in the tension between the church and the world. If they are, in this situation, to perceive, accept, and fulfill the gospel, every means must be employed to help them to grasp it in all its implications.

To those outside the church's fellowship the gospel must also be communicated by every available means, that they too may perceive, accept, and fulfill it, if that be God's will.

THE GOSPEL AND EDUCATION

One of the ministries by which the church communicates the gospel to its members and to those outside is the ministry of teaching. The teaching function of the church is:

1. To deliver the message that in man's extreme need God has forgiven and redeemed him in Jesus Christ.   This is urgent.

2. To help those inside and those outside the church to prepare themselves for response to that message.

3. To show them how to respond.

4. To help them to see and work out the fullness of the implications of the message of the gospel for themselves and their world.

If one way by which the church communicates the gospel is by teaching, then the gospel is of central concern to Christian education. Because it sustains such a vital relationship to the church's teaching ministry, there are certain specific connections between the gospel and Christian education that can be pointed out, bringing the whole matter into focus at this point.

Christian education (defined in the fullest sense to include the church and the Christian home) has a task of preparation for response, demonstration of how to respond, and guidance in mature response as it seeks to make persons aware of their living encounter with the gospel. In *In One Spirit* (p. 17; Friendship Press, 1958) I put it this way:

"The individual has his choice. He may remain in tragic bondage to self, society, and culture. This is what is meant by "the human predicament. On the other hand he may become a free person, by God's Spirit, through his response in complete devotion to Jesus Christ. Christian education seeks to prepare the individual to respond in faith by the power of the Holy Spirit, to show him how he may respond to the living Word as it is spoken to him, and to guide him into increasingly mature and effective ways of responding to the Holy Spirit and doing the Father's will. This is why Christian education is called the nurture of the Christian life." (Used by permission.)

The emphasis is clearly on how one becomes a free person through response to the gospel.

This, in turn, makes it even more evident than before that Christian education in the church (again, using the term in the fullest sense) is responsible for assisting persons to perceive the gospel the gospel, to accept it, and to see its demands and fulfill them. There is never a time in a person's life or in the life of the church when any one of these aspects may be separated from the other two, but it is helpful in seeing the church's educational task with persons of different levels of experience to point out that in childhood the emphasis is likely to be more on perceiving the gospel, in youth on accepting it, and in maturity on discovering and meeting its ever-changing requirements.

Thus Christian education definitely implies the closest attention to the gospel and to its work at every point. When we examine the objectives of Christian education we will see them in the light of the gospel. When we look at educational procedures, it will be chiefly in the context of the gospel. And when we describe the educational programs and institutions involved (including church and home), the major concern will be with communicating the gospel and nurturing faithful discipleship in the light of it.

Christian education is inextricably bound up with the gospel, but what of education in general? Here, again, some things that have been said before come into focus. Education has to be concerned with helping persons to see things as they are and to come to grips with life. Its indispensable emphasis is on human becoming--the development of free and mature persons. We have seen how the various aspects of so-called secular education--technical education, liberal education, and moral and religious education--can be carried on in the light of the gospel if the learner approaches them from a fully Christian perspective. Something of the results of that approach in increased insights, higher achievement of competence, and a greater sense of having come to terms with life, have been hinted at.

The teacher in so-called secular education, as well as the learner, can do his work within a Christian perspective. If the gospel is what it claims to be, it involves living relationships and a quality of life even more than it does the use of any particular words or the expression of any particular sectarian ideas. The teacher who, in a secular school, lives and teaches in the assurance of God's redeeming love for him in Jesus Christ, provides a living witness that needs no special words in the classroom. Such a teacher need not, indeed cannot, hide who he is, how he became what he is, what he does as a result, and what it means to him. His whole life, from personal devotions to responsible social action, girds him for his witness.

But the words themselves need not be missing. They cannot be the subject of exhortation in the public classroom. Yet it is the responsibility of every teacher, and especially teachers of subjects dealing with the expression of human needs and values, to point out, among the various approaches to the problems of life, the fact that there is a Christian gospel, and that it provides a distinctive approach to understanding and dealing with human problems.

These are some of the relationships of the gospel to education--both church education and education in general. Consideration of these relationships has brought us to the place where we can summarize the possibility of the gospel as the criterion for education. Is it adequate? Is it simple? Is it clear?

The gospel provides an adequate basis for guiding Christian education because it is integral to the Word of God, because it is the clue to the meaning of history, because it is the clue to the meaning of existence, because it brings the church into existence and gives it its imperative, and because (in educational terms) it is the clue to human becoming.

The gospel provides a simple basis for the guidance of Christian education because, for all its profundity, it may be put in a simple proposition (God's redeeming work on man's behalf in Jesus Christ) and in concrete terms (as concrete as the manger, the teacher, the healer, the cross, and the empty tomb) without losing anything really essential.

The gospel provides a clear basis for the guidance of Christian education because it is easily and readily understandable at many different educational and experience levels.

THE GUIDING PRINCIPLE STATED

Conceived as a principle that may be used to assist and guide in the development of objectives, curriculum principles, and principles of administration, this center and focus on the gospel in Christian education may be stated thus:

If Christian education will focus its attention on the gospel, it will be properly oriented and conceived. Around the gospel the other elements of Christian education may be grouped, but it is the one element that can stand alone and give the others meaning. The gospel is the essential element in establishing the institutions of Christian education and devising their curriculums.

Here then, in the form of a guiding principle, is summarized the conviction that the central concern of, and norm for, the educational life and work of the church is the gospel--in all its implications for the revelation of God, for the nature and condition of man, for the meaning of history, for individual and social salvation and responsibility, for the significance and mission of the church, and for the fulfillment of human destiny.

* * * * * * * * * *

C. Ellis Nelson
(1967)

[From *Where Faith Begins* (Richmond: John Knox Press, 1967), pp. 183-198.]

As indicated in the first chapter, there is no obvious, utilitarian connection between a theory of communication and the practical problems in the church. Matters such as the size of a church school class or the use of mechanical aids in teaching may be related to a theory of communication; but in actual practice almost all theories use the same methods. The way in which a method or a mechanical aid is used may be influenced by your theory of communication. Preaching is a good illustration. Religious groups of all types in the whole spectrum of the Judeo-Christian tradition use preaching; but the way it is used by the Quakers is different from the use made by Presbyterians, by leaders of a revivalist sect, or by the Roman Catholic Church. A theory helps us set goals for our work, suggests a starting place, gives us a basis for allocating our time and money to various means of communication, and provides a basis for judging our effectiveness. In short, a theory should help us find guidelines for our work.

Throughout this book I have used the general term "community of believers" in order to focus attention on the communal nature of the Christian faith and to avoid any hard-and-fast identification with the institutionalized church. God's Spirit has on many occasions broken out of established institutional structures to form new communities and new ways of worship and service, and we must assume that this may be happening now. However, the local congregation has been a characteristic form of the church since New testament times; therefore, in this brief discussion of a model I shall have in mind a local congregation.

THE CENTRALITY OF THE CONGREGATION

Our major mistake in Protestantism has been the assumption--made especially acute by the rise of the religious education movement at the beginning of the twentieth century--that the communication of faith was, in the greater part, directly dependent upon classroom instruction of children and youth. This is not the place to analyze that situation in detail, but we are now aware that Protestants are in a state of crisis in relation to educational strategy. In brief, our present strategy was formed during the period when a Protestant ethos characterized our nation. Under such circumstances, the Sunday school and other part-time voluntary agencies of instruction were satisfactory. Now, in an era of radical pluralism in which we have a wide variety of religious groups and a large secular or humanist group, we Protestants find that the basic strategy developed over a century ago is inadequate for the cultural situation in which we live.

The first thing we have to do in this approach is to remove from our minds the notion that the communication of the Christian faith is directly dependent upon any instructional agencies or methods and fix in our minds the idea that faith is fostered by a community of believers, usually a congregation. Instruction is a necessary part of the life of the congregation, but instruction must be related to the life of the congregation. Along with this shift of focus from the instructional agencies of the congregation to the congregation itself, we must abandon our cherished American individualism. Education--especially that of children--is always focused on the individual; yet this can be done without making the individual the center of the educational process. We can excuse the nineteenth-century Protestant for his individualism because of the frontier situation in that era and because the social sciences had not yet developed an understanding of the process of socialization. Today, we must return to the Biblical view that a person is the product of his culturing group.

We start then with the congregation as the primary society of Christians and say that life together is the method and the quality of what is communicated. This is a description of as process, and it is important to separate this process from what we think ought to be communicated; but until we get this process in mind we cannot make much use of this approach. A sleepy rural church that grinds through a traditional program teaches that Christianity is a set of beliefs and customs. A small remnant of white Protestants in a large, ornate imitation Gothic building located in what was once a fashionable neighborhood but is now called an "inner-city situation" is demonstrating its beliefs when it maintains a clublike gathering of people with similar backgrounds and personal interests. Contrariwise, a congregation that is seriously searching for God's leading, made up of individuals who are consciously coaching each other on ways they can actualize their ministry for Christ in their community, communicates their yearning as well as their interpretation of Christianity.

This proposition seems so simple to me that I feel embarrassed to record it. However, on many occasions when I have voiced this idea to ministers, most will agree; but after a whole one will say, "You know the trouble in my church is the Sunday school, and I must do something about it. Where can I get a better curriculum?" Then after waiting a few minutes until the meaning of my question has become clear, I continue, What would be different in your church if you ordered your printed instructional materials from a different address?" This question does not solve the problem. Yet, it forces the questioner to see that the human community is the place where one must start and that printed curriculum materials can support but can seldom create change.

After seeing that the group of believers is the unit with which we must work, we must then see that whatever is done or said, or not done or not said, *is* teaching. There is no such thing as postponing the solution to a problem. The decision to postpone is a decision; it teaches that the issue is too hot to handle, that such issues are not appropriate for the church, or that the tactic of postponement is more important at this point than a resolution to settle the matter. People learn from the way events are handled. There is no neutrality. If a congregation attempts to be neutral, it teaches that on the issues at hand it can't make up its mind, it is fearful of the result of a decision, or it is confused about how to proceed. There is no avoidance of an issue. Not to see an issue is to teach that Christians do not see issues. Christians who avoid problems in social ethics--such as involvement in racial relations, war, or the distribution of wealth--are saying that

the Christian faith does not operate in these areas. We must
see the congregation as a field of forces--individuals and
groups--in lively interaction with each other; the grist of this
interactional process *is* the content of their faith. We must
see the congregation as a force in a field of other forces in
the community. What the congregation as a group says and
does in the community is the meaning they give to their faith.
If we practice our theology within this interactive frame of
reference, we will then be able to see that the functions of
worship, searching (study), development of ethical positions
on issues, and ministry to the community are all sui)ordinate
to the congregation's purpose of being the people of God in a
certain time and place.

INTERPRETATION--THE DOMINANT ACTIVITY

In order to be the people of God, the congregation must
see itself as living in a stream of interpreted history. This
approach keeps us from falling into the commonly held
notion that the Christian faith is an absolute which we
discover with the help of our theology and then apply to
situations we face. Christianity-in this latter sense-is an
abstraction, ~and our efforts to apply it usually take the form
of saying what we think should be done without any serious
consideration of whether it actually can be done. Rather, we
must see ourselves as interpreting a tradition that was in its
day an interpretation. The reality with which we must work
is the community of believers; in order to gain perspective on
ourselves we need constantly to go back to the experiences
which other generations have had with God in order to
understand how God works through his church and through
the world of human events. We cannot get a perspective
without comparison. We cannot know God except as we
know how other generations responded to him.

To identify the congregation s dominant activity as
interpretation forces us   to focus attention on   the

interactional process as well as on the tradition we have received. We have to see that the unique aspect of our relation with each other is our faith, regardless of how weak or immature it may be; that we learn to receive the gift of grace as we practice it in relation to each other; that the ties of affection we have with each other are the only foundation which will support our differences of opinion; and that as a group we have to search for the meaning of our faith in the past and then test it in the present. This process is a long way from the method of applying intellectual formulation to specific problems.

The congregation, then, is a school of faith. All that the congregation does is both a means of communicating the faith and a subject of investigation. This must not be taken to the extreme by the congregations so that they become "paralyzed by analysis," but this is not likely to happen in America. The opposite is most likely the case--the congregation becoming tradition-bound. It is that condition we must fight.

How can we avoid being tradition-bound yet honor our tradition? We must subject our activities to systematic study and make appropriate changes. Worship, for example, is something that we do every Sunday according to a traditional pattern; yet seldom does a congregation know why we have the pattern, much less that it might be changed. Every aspect of worship could be the subject of investigation. At the end of a year or two, some new forms might be developed and new ways of congregational participation be evolved, or else the old ones might be retained because they are better understood. The sacraments are seldom explained except to the confirmation classes, yet we use them constantly. It is important for adults, who often have only a vague idea of what the Lord's Supper means or who have lost their sense of the meaning of the ritual, to have a chance to look afresh at the way this sacrament came into being. In some areas it would be a shock to Christians to learn that Jesus used wine and not Welch's grape juice. From that trivial fact they could start to learn how their own American pietistic tradition had interpreted the bible; thus, in small ways they might begin to develop a historical perspective which should mature so that they could become able to transpose the meaning of other events from the first to the twentieth century.

These standard elements of worship are a good illustration of the problems we face. Normally, the child at confirmation receives a theologically correct definition of the traditional belief about worship and sacraments, and there the matter lies for the rest of his life. Unless the child is unusually inquisitive, he gets no further instruction except what may come incidentally in communion sermons. His mind is religiously arrested at the teen-age level. But the child grows, his mind expands, experiences that were anticipated (such as vocation, marriage, parenthood) become personal to him; yet, his understanding of the Christian faith remains where it was when he was a young teen-ager. The congregation needs to continue to interpret its worship and sacraments to the growing person on through the life cycle, deepening and enriching their meaning as the person becomes more capable of responding to the depths of understanding which are conveyed by the symbols in the sacrament.

Along with this need for the congregation to continually interpret its worship to members at various maturity levels, the congregation needs to interpret the nature and the ministry of the church to its members, especially to new members. The way in which the normal Protestant church receives adult members is a reliable guide to what that church is. Too often the process is casual: no more is demanded of the prospective member than that he show an interest in religion or certify that in the past he belonged to a congregation somewhere. Whatever meaning the Christian faith has must be made manifest as a part of the act of joining. There are few times in the life of a person when education can be as effective as at the time of joining a church. Let me repeat the saying of Kurt Lewin, "Learning is first a new belonging." The congregation must maintain a comprehensive, educational plan for receiving new members. This would include vigorous study for at least three months, the act of joining, and a continuation of training for at least three more months so that the individual may find ways to minister in the name of Christ. This latter segment of membership training is almost totally absent from Protestant church life today. If the congregation is the community of believers, then we must make the act of joining an integral part of the process of "belonging." It is *after* a person has made a decision that he is psychologically most open to an explanation of the fullest meaning of his decision. If the decision has any significance at all, he tests that decision in his daily round of activities to see what difference that new belonging makes.

We must move into this natural, psychological state and help the new member find his ministry, or else we teach (remember there is no neutrality!) that membership consists of just "going to church." We cannot honestly say to church members that they should have a ministry unless we help them find such a ministry. The problem is as old as 1 Corinthians 12-13. We would agree with Paul that people have a variety of gifts, and that they should find the way they can use their gifts for the upbuilding of the body of Christ while they also find and practice the more "excellent way" of love in human relations. But we must define "belonging" so that a person makes a conscious decision about what he will do with his personal gifts in a particular ministry. We should be as practical and concrete about this aspect of belonging as we are about explaining the budget and handing the new member a pledge card to sign!

The budget of the congregation is a theological statement of belief. The budget may have more power to convey the real beliefs of the congregation than the educational program, and we should spend more time developing the budget so that a wide representation of the members can participate in its planning. The standard items all need more attention. Is the percentage of the budget for creature comforts for the congregation out of line with what is used in a ministry to the community? To state the question that way raises the question of the role of the church in the community. Should the church pay taxes for what it receives from the community? If not taxes, should the church pay a token amount in lieu of taxes to demonstrate that it wants to help carry the cost of education, police, fire protection? Should the church set up a child guidance clinic, or use its facilities for tutoring student dropouts? Questions of the church's proper function come alive in the budget preparation, and such questions should be encouraged and made the subject of investigations. We should raise questions such as these: Is this proposed expenditure appropriate to the ministry in Christ which we as a church are attempting in this community? Is our congregation the proper one to do this, or should we coordinate our work with some other agency or churches? to ask these and related questions is to open up an awareness of what the congregation may do to be an extension of Christ's ministry in the world. *Not* to ask this type of question is to reinforce the notion that the budget is only an organized way to pay running expenses and that the church has little interest in events taking place around it.

The buildings and physical surroundings of the congregation provide more data about the beliefs which really function within the life of the congregation. Buildings are solidified ideas. If the congregation has attempted to build a cathedral--allocating its attention to all of the details necessary to erect and maintain this type of edifice--it must in all honesty label the building a museum or a pride symbol. Sunday school lessons on humility have little meaning in a congregation that is spending most of its time and money on a building as a status symbol: what is learned under such circumstances is that a person should appear to be modest while he struggles to impress other people. The physical location and the character of the church property all say something about the beliefs of the congregation. Perhaps we should rethink the whole matter of holding property, for most of our waste is at this point. We have billions of dollars invested in buildings that are seldom used. A congregation ought to consider whether its living of the faith cannot be done more appropriately in rented buildings, in buildings shared with congregations of other faiths, or in commercial buildings that are idle on weekends. The churches of America could preach an unforgettable sermon by cashing in much of their property, moving to less pretentious quarters, and using that money in their ministry.

We could go on and discuss the administrative policies of the congregation or the salary schedule of employees as illustrating how the local congregation in its life lives an interpretation of the tradition it proclaims, but additional areas for examination are not necessary. It may be necessary to say again that this interpretation by the congregation of its functions is not something we add, nor is it a program to be superimposed on activities already going on; it is a normal and necessary part of the congregational life. The only issues before us are whether we will be aware of the process of communication that is going on by reason of the choices our congregation makes and whether we will deliberately use these choices to reflect the meaning of our faith.

THE SHAPING OF MENTALITY

We started with the most obvious and visible aspects of congregational life to illustrate the inevitability of the congregation's interpreting the meaning of faith in relation to its life as an institution in the community. Now we must look closely at the more deliberate efforts of the Christian community to form the mentality of its members: preaching and teaching.

Since this is not an essay on homiletics, the sermon as such will not be discussed except to say that it is one of the principal means of interpreting the contemporary meaning of the Christian faith and therefore the shaping of the mentality of Christians. In the average Protestant church the minister is the only trained interpreter of tradition, and he is the principal leader of the congregation's life. Sermons reach more of the adults of the congregation than any other efforts to interpret the Christian message, so we start with them.

Different religious traditions interpret the role of the sermon differently. These interpretations range from that of the Quakers, who have no formal sermon, to that of the Presbyterians and Lutherans, who often insist that the sermon is the contemporary word of God. All traditions that use the sermon consider it to be contemporary speech about God in the light of the past, regardless of how effective it is expected to be for the present. My personal feeling is that the sermon can be a useful way to mold Christian mentality but that it can be more effective if it is considered a part of the ongoing life of the congregation than if it is a feature of the worship or the principal activity of the minister. To consider the sermon a part of the ongoing life of the congregation would require a basic reformulation of the method by which sermons are planned and used.

The normal method is for the minister to preach on whatever topics seem right to him. He may use topics appropriate to the liturgical year, special events in the community, or problems that arise in the congregation. Once preached, the sermon has completed its usefulness except for occasional mimeographing for wider distribution. I believe we must maintain the autonomy of the pulpit and must create a climate of opinion which will support the right of the minister to preach on whatever topic seems appropriate to him. Freedom of the pulpit--like academic freedom in the university--will be abused, but in the long run it is the only way for a prophetic voice to be heard. A minister should approach his preaching with the reverence that is appropriate for such an important task. Whatever weaknesses he may have in preparation and training, he is responsible to God for whatever he says. It is for this reason that I do not believe it is appropriate to have a discussion of the sermon soon after its delivery; this plan sets up a situation where the minister becomes too conscious of his auditors, nor does it give them enough time to brood over the sermon.

A better plan would be to see the sermon as the minister's unique part in a variety of interpreted actions participated in by the congregation during the week. When he was a minister in a church in the East Harlem Protestant parish, George W. Webber developed a lectionary of Biblical passages to be used through the week by all of the groups in the church. On Wednesday nights, adults and church school teachers in home meetings went over the passage with commentaries to find its meaning for their situation, and on Sunday that passage was the Biblical reference for the sermon. Other groups meeting at other times, including the church school, also used the selected passage for the week. The congregation by searching the Scripture in a variety of ways had some sense of unity as God's people and of mutual interdependence in finding God's word of guidance for themselves. This or some similar arrangement makes the shaping of a Christian mentality the first order of business for the whole congregation rather than just for the educational specialists or the ordained clergy; yet the sermon and the church school class each has its distinct place.

The sermon can be built into the ongoing life of the congregation in other ways. A youth group or adult group could request a series of sermons on a particular subject and ask for copies for discussion purposes. If the minister is not present for the discussion, the group should summarize their reactions to the sermon and send them to him.

Today there is no liturgical reason why laymen should not participate in the worship, leading various parts or composing prayers. The minister might for symbolic purpose come down into the congregation for pastoral prayers or ask for various concerns that should be incorporated in the pastoral prayers. The announcement period does not have to be a recital of information already mimeographed in the church bulletin and held in everyone's hands.   The announcements could consist of brief comments about the program or problems the church is having in its various ministries. It could be important to hear a news report from some church group, a recounting of an insight into a Biblical passage which has appeared spontaneously in a class, or an enumeration of the docket faced by the official board with a request for prayers for guidance, a short account of an event involving the way some church met a difficult problem creatively, or an excerpt from a soldier's letter describing what he was up against on the battlefield, and so on. There are many ways a congregation can keep itself informed about its ongoing life rather than concentrating on organizational machinery.

DEVELOPING CRITICAL INTELLIGENCE

Part of the shaping of Christian mentality is the development of critical intelligence. Although all aspects of congregational life contribute to the shaping, the role is normally played by organized study groups. This approach to communication would insist that our strategy in formal, educational work start with, and be centered in, the communicant members of the church. This is so because adults are the people responsible for the decisions which make the congregation what it is, they are the influential agencies in the home and society, and they are the only ones with enough maturity to evaluate the tradition critically. Such an approach is different from the strategy formed in the early nineteenth century by evangelical theology which assumed that the Sunday school was a preparation for conversion or for membership in the church. This approach is different from the strategy formed in the early twentieth century by the liberal religious educator who, with his new psychological understanding of the child, wanted to make personal experience the center of the religious education process. Both of these strategies were child-centered and highly individualistic.

This approach--the congregation as the primary society and faith in God as the goal--requires adult believers to be the agents of communication in all relationships and assumes that the range of awareness and quality of life cannot go much beyond where the adults are in their spiritual discernment. While the strategy centers on adults, its purpose is to help adults live, test, and modify the Christian tradition to fit situations they are facing. Enough has been said in previous chapters about the kind of interpretation that must go on in order to live the tradition, so we shall simply indicate here a variety of practical ways this can be done in a Protestant congregation.

We should face realistically the major problem involved in any effort to train the laity of a congregation. Adults are not like children. They already have acquired the basic patterns of thought, action, and skills necessary to carry on their life. They do not readily see the need for any organized serious study of religion. They may see the need for study related to their profession, for such study helps them advance in their work. But their religious development too often has been arrested back in childhood. Because their deep and often unconscious emotions are related to the attitudes their parents had and the way their parents implanted a conscience within them, they cannot easily open this area of their life to the rational processes of the mind. That is why adults are so defensive or aggressive in the church when some idea or proposal runs counter to the older and deeper emotionalized attitudes that occupy the substructure of their personality. Also, many adults had unfortunate experiences with classroom instruction in their childhood. They were caught in a competitive situation where they could not excel, they were graded unfairly, or most likely they saw little connection between organized study and the human problems they had to solve. The average adult is a battle-scarred veteran in classroom instruction, so he is wary of additional group study.

It is also true that some of the adults in a church will have had good experiences in classroom instruction in the past and will be eager to continue to grow in their understanding of religion. The rapid expansion of departments of religion in state and independent universities and the large enrollment in these classes indicate a seriousness about religion and a desire to explore religious questions. This generation of young people will be in our churches in a few years to enrich the number of young adults who have had a taste of what education in religion can be. We must provide opportunity for these people to continue to probe the meaning of religion and must use them as yeast to permeate the body of conventional Christians who are apprehensive about serious study.

These comments are made to dispel any notion that, if we just reverse the strategy of the Sunday school and of the liberal religious education movement and focus attention on adults rather than on children, we automatically will solve our problem of communicating faith. We will indeed have a strategy which will allow the natural socialization process to work effectively, but we cannot assume that adults will respond to the same educational efforts we have learned to use for children and youth. Although there is an accumulated body of material about how adults learn when they are motivated by economic necessity, we do not have a clear understanding of how adults learn in informal, voluntary associations such as the church; nor do we have dependable knowledge of how adults change their values and world view except as it is done in relation to the primary societies to which they give allegiance. So we are in a situation which requires that we change our basic strategy, but we are not able to offer assurance that any particular program of adult education will be satisfactory.

We must therefore reassure ourselves that the congregational approach is, in spite of all its difficulties, the one that makes progress--even though it is the advance of the turtle rather than of the jack rabbit. Once we have made that determination, then we can see all the natural structures of the congregation as possibilities for enlightenment, expansion of awareness, and education. We will have great flexibility in our approach to education if we make short-range plans and if we are able to try many different ways of education--depending on the situation in the congregation, the age, maturity, and educational background of the communicant members, the general characteristics of the community, and the special needs of the believers.

I am, therefore, reluctant to make specific suggestions for fear that they will be followed! For a congregation to start an adult education effort on the basis of what worked somewhere else is wrong. They may actually end up doing some of the things other congregations do; but if they bypass an examination of their own situation, they will be using a prescription without identifying the disease. Remember that Paul did not write 1 Corinthians 13 because he thought love was a noble sentiment but because it was the only antidote for the quarreling of rival parties, their lack of respect for each other, their drunkenness and selfishness, which were described in chapters 11 and 12. Through a committee or official board, a congregation must bring to the surface the value structure which is shared by its members, and then it can make plans to discuss those values. Otherwise, congregations deal with the racial relations problem as if it were a problem only in South Africa. Or, they use their underlying competitive attitude to enhance the church's reputation in the community in every measurable item, such as size of budget, number of members, or quality of organ; these become the criteria of success. Unless the value structure itself is treated, study of the Christian tradition will be only a mental exercise or else it will be twisted to support the social values already accepted.

In some churches, it would be possible to organize a group of adults to teach themselves by having a common textbook or an agreement that a certain book of the Bible plus certain commentaries were to be used. Such groups, numbering about twenty in size, would assign to couples or small groups the sections to be studied so that each session would start with a report from these studies. There should be a leader for the discussion. Such a self-taught group could start off by selecting areas to be investigated, such as modern art and what it says for man? 5 condition. Another group might undertake to find out what the local Jewish people thought about problems among their people. Another could seek to make connections with the nearest Catholic church and find out how the changes proposed at Vatical Council II were working out and what they thought were the major problems in Catholic-Protestant relations in that community. Other task groups could investigate the way juvenile delinquency was handled in the community or what the minority racial groups believed to be the barriers to, and possibilities for, good relations within the community. By properly scheduling these reports and by allowing six to eight weeks for discussion of each area investigated, an adult group could use a year in delving deeply into the nature of contemporary man and the human situation in which he lives.

With this basic proposition in mind, we review briefly a few other specific opportunities for adults to search the tradition for contemporary meaning. All congregations have official groups in charge of the management and various phases of the church's work. If thirty to forty minutes of the official board's meeting time could be scheduled for organized study of the Bible or for topics related to their work, the study function could become a normal part of administration without adding any extra meetings. Christian education committees could profitably study the theories of Christian education or the relation of the church to public education; or they could devise ways to test the Biblical understanding of the congregation in order to bring the church school teaching closer to the interpreted motifs which are already operating in the congregation. Perhaps we should *require* that all of our official boards budget a third of their time for study. Such a rule would dramatize the fact that individuals are agents of communication and that they must continually develop their understanding of Christianity in order to be effective as persons in the office through which they are serving.

In some congregations, short-term study groups by occupation are helpful, for there are few places where doctors, lawyers, and businessmen can gather to discuss the ethical decisions they face every day. These groups should not be allowed to solidify into permanent subunits; that would prevent a sharing of religious experience throughout the congregation, which is essential to its well-being.

There should be short-term training courses to help the laity perfect its ministry. We are counseled from the pulpit that we ought to do certain things; through church publications we are inundated with suggestions from our national boards about things we ought to be doing; and we can observe conditions in the community which the church could modify and improve, yet seldom is any guidance given as to how these things might be done. Thus, we only heighten the sense of guilt which comes from not doing what we ought to do. Our finest learning comes when we have to face situations as Christian persons, and our joy in serving comes when we do what we know how to do. These can be linked when we help people learn how to minister. Visiting the sick is an illustration. Not everyone has this ability; but there are fundamental elements in visitation, including the use of Scripture and prayer, that can be taught. A group formed on this basis should practice its ministry and report back to the larger group the experiences its members are having, discussing how the conditions thus reported are to be handled. Out of these reports will come some of the most perplexing and common human experiences such as grief, guilt, need of reassurance; all of these should be topics of study by the training group. I mention visitation because it is one of the most obvious ministries that a community of believers can maintain, and also to show how such a group can be a springboard into a study of some of the most profound religious problems.

Training groups can be formed about many areas of ministry, such as social action, community service, teaching in the church school, or tutoring public school children. But it is essential that these groups not learn a few methods of work and then be dismissed to perform this ministry on their own. It is imperative that the people involved in practicing their ministry bring back to their group in the church for discussion and further study the experiences and problems they are having. It is in this kind of study and participation that we are forced to learn and through which we formulate meaning.

The congregation should give more attention to the ways (in addition to public worship) everyone can be engaged in common study in response to common themes or seasons. Perhaps Advent and Lent offer the best possibilities for a coordinated effort of study, from four to six weeks in length. Through preaching, common Bible study, plays, art exhibits, films, and ungraded discussion groups a series of topics can be studied which will enrich everyone's experience and help demonstrate that the congregation is made up of people of various ages, vocations, educational attainments, and abilities. Such occasions need to be carefully planned by a representative group so that the various parts fit the needs of the congregation, rather than being just an assemblage of programs topically arranged which people are invited to attend. If a play is enacted, it should be related to the general theme. Time should be scheduled for a thorough discussion of it in all of the church school classes or adult groups the next Sunday.

We have come this far before mentioning adult Bible study classes in order to show that congregational education can

operate in a variety of ways other than formal adults classes. Classes of this nature are important and should be continued. In spite of the weakness of the traditional adult Bible class, it has been--in many congregations--the only effort toward adult education which Sunday by Sunday required adults to read the Bible and ponder its meaning.   Many suggestions have been made to improve the teaching and diversity the subject matter of these classes.   The main problem is to prevent their getting in a rut. When an adult class runs along the same path for a number of years, it becomes more a~ more the means of satisfying the social needs of the members rather than an effort to understand the Bible.   In order to make the whole congregation the primary society, adult study groups should be formed and reformed annually with new combinations of teachers, adults, and curriculum.

Notes

[1]For a suggestive exposition of democratic religion as over against individualist and imperialist types of religion, see W. A. Brown, Imperialistic Religion and the Religion of Democracy (New York, 1923), Chap. v.

[2]Anders Nygren goes so far as to say "that the idea of the infinite value of the human soul is not a basic Christian idea at all." Agape and Eros (Eng. tr., London, 1932), p. 55.

[3]Cf. G. A. Coe, Psychology of Religion (Chicago, 1916), p. 250.

[4]Ibid., p. 252.

[5]Ibid., p. 240.

[6]Ibid., p. 244.

[7]Ibid., pp. 237-245.

[8]Bearing of Psychology upon Religion (New York, 1916), p. 75.

[9]Coe, Psychology of Religion, p. 242.

[10]What Is Christian Education? (New York, 1929), p. 76.

[11]William C. Bower, The Curriculum of Religious Education (New York, 1925), p. 234.

[12]Ibid., p. 237.

[13]"A Theology Relevant to Religious Education," Religious Education, xxxiv (1939), p. 201.

[14]"My Own Little Theatre," in Religion in Transition, p. 106. Italics added. For a similar point of view voiced by a group of prominent religious educators, see W. C. Bower, et al., "The Nature and Function of Religion," Religious Education, xxxi (1936), p. 97.

[15]Cf. Charles A. Ellwood, The Reconstruction of Religion (New York, 1922), pp. 39-42, 125-126.

[16]"My Own Little Theatre," in Religion in Transition, p. 109. In his What Is Christian Education?, p. 268, Coe says: "We ourselves must make a new demonstration of ethical love in human relations, or else lose our faith in God."

[17]Cf. Henri Bergson, The Two Sources of Morality and Religion (Eng. tr., London, 19325), p. 67.

[18]In his Reconstruction of Religion, Charles A. Ellwood says: "Modern democracy is essentially a movement to realize the ideals of social religion; and all genuine social religion is necessarily a religion of democracy." P. 249.

[19]"The next step in the development of an ethical theology," wrote Gerald B. Smith in 1913, "must be the translation of the categories of divinity into terms compatible with democratic ethics." Social Idealism and the Changing Theology (New York, 1913), p. 228.

[20]A Social Theory of Religious Education, p. 55.

[21]The Curriculum of Religious Education, p. 237. Italics added.

[22]Educating for Citizenship (New York, 1932), p. 143.

[23]Loc. cit.

[24]Ibid., p. 186.

The Quest for Meaning

Philip Phenix

It is impossible to read Philip Phenix, recent professor of philosophy and education at Teachers College, without being forcefully reminded of Maurus. While some one thousand years separate these men, the issues are basically the same: the nature of truth, the definition of education, the relationship between gospel and culture, and an underlying understanding of the marks of the educated Christian. It is not overstatement to suggest that Phenix presented the most wholistic inter-disciplinary approach to the curriculum of religious education in the twentieth century

The seven liberal arts are commonly recognized in the Latin words *trivium* and *quadrivium*. The *trivium* pointed to the verbal arts: grammar, rhetoric, and logic or dialectic. The *quadrivium* pointed to the mathematical arts: arithmetic, music, geometry, and astronomy. Given birth in the ancient Greek culture, and eventually assimilated by Rome, the seven liberal arts were more than a random collection of curriculum content areas. They embodied, rather, the very cultural inheritance and ethos of the ancient Western world.[1] Said another way, these seven liberal arts embodied the core values of a particular cultural group. The very act of teaching the seven-fold curriculum, then, was a powerful and carefully delineated means of perpetuating taken-for-granted ideological systems from one generation to the next. In short, rather than an haphazard combination of knowledge areas, the seven

liberal arts contained within them a precise culturally patterned answer
to the question, "What does it mean to be human?"

As Maurus, Phenix did not seek to divorce "secular" knowledge from
"sacred" knowledge. The two following selections are taken from
Phenix's best known works, *Realms of Meaning* and *Education and the
Worship of God*. The former dealt with general education, and the
latter with religious education. A careful reading of the following
selections, however, reveals that for Phenix, all true education is
fundamentally religious.

* * * * * * * * * *

Philip Phenix

(1964)

[From *Realms of Meaning: A Philosophy of the Curriculum for
General Education* (New York: McGraw-Hill Book Company, 1964),
pp. 3-8.]

It is not easy to sustain a sense of the whole. Many a
person pursues his own limited calling with scarcely a
thought for his place in the total drama of civilized endeavor.
While he may have a vague notion of the larger context in
which his contribution is made, he may never engage in any
sustained study and reflection about his relation to the entire
pattern of civilization.

This limitation of outlook is evident even in education. All
too commonly the teacher teaches a particular subject or unit
within a subject without any reference to its relationships to
other components of the curriculum. Similarly, the student
may study one subject after another with no idea of what his
growing fund of knowledge and skill might contribute to an
integrated way of life. Students and teachers alike are prone
to take the curriculum as they find it, as a traditional
sequence of separate elements, without ever inquiring into
the comprehensive pattern within which the constituent parts
are located.

Since education is the means of perpetuating culture from
generation to generation, it is natural that the partiality of
outlook endemic in the culture generally would be found also
in education. Yet, this consequence need not follow.

Indeed, the special office of education is to widen one's view of life, to deepen insight into relationships, and to counteract the provincialism of customary existence--in short, to engender an integrated outlook.

If this integral perspective is to be attained, a philosophy of the curriculum is necessary. By such a philosophy is meant a critically examined, coherent system of ideas by which all the constituent parts of the course of instruction are identified and ordered.

A unitary philosophy of the curriculum is important for many reasons, among which the following four may be cited: First, comprehensive outlook is necessary for all intelligent decisions about what shall be included and excluded from the course of study. If one subject is to be chosen instead of another, it is important to know how the one differs from the other and why the one is to be preferred to the other as a constituent in the complete pattern of the learner's experience and character.

Second, because a person is essentially an organized totality and not just a collection of separate parts, the curriculum ought to have a corresponding organic quality. Since it is one and the same person who undergoes each of the successive experiences in his course of study, the plan of study can best contribute to the person's growth if it is governed by the goal of wholeness for the human being.

Third, society, as well as individual persons, depends upon principles of community; corporate life, like the life of each individual, requires some overall plan. A curriculum planned as a comprehensive design for learning contributes a basis for the growth of community, while an atomized program of studies engenders disintegration in the life of society.

Fourth, a comprehensive concept of the structure of learning gives added significance to each of the component segments of the curriculum. The value of any subject is enhanced by an understanding of its relationships with other subjects, and its distinctive features are best comprehended in the light of its similarities and contrasts with other subjects.

The purpose of the present work is to sketch a view of the curriculum for general education by showing how the desirable scope, content, and arrangement of studies may be derived from certain fundamental considerations about human nature and knowledge. it will be shown that the controlling idea of general education, imparting unity to the pattern of studies, emerges from a philosophy of man and his ways of knowing.

The main line of argument may be summarized as follows:

Human beings are essentially creatures who have the power to experience *meanings*. Distinctively human existence consists in a pattern of meanings. Furthermore, *general education is the process of engendering essential meanings*.

Unfortunately, the pathway to the fulfillment of meaning is never smooth. The human situation is such that mankind is always threatened by forces that destroy achievements and give way all too readily to attitudes of futility, frustration, and doubt. Meaning is thus lost in an abyss of meaninglessness.

The perennial threat to meaning is intensified under the conditions of modern industrial civilization. Four contributing factors deserve special emphasis. The first is the spirit of criticism and skepticism. This spirit is part of the scientific heritage, but it has also tended to bring the validity of all meanings into question. The second factor is the pervasive depersonalization and fragmentation of life caused by the extreme specialization of a complex, interdependent society. The third factor is the sheer mass of cultural products, especially knowledge, which modern man is required to assimilate. The fourth factor is the rapid rate of change in the conditions of life, resulting in a pervasive feeling of impermanence and insecurity.

Since the object of general education is to lead to the fulfillment of human life through the enlargement and deepening of meaning, the modern curriculum should be designed with particular attention to these sources of meaninglessness in contemporary life. That is to say, the curriculum should be planned so as to counteract destructive skepticism, depersonalization and fragmentation, overabundance, and transience.

If education is to be regarded as grounded in the search for meaning, the primary goal of a philosophy of the curriculum is to analyze the nature of meaning. Meaningful experience is of many kinds; there is no single quality that may be designated as the one essence of meaning. Accordingly, we should speak not of meaning as such, but of meanings, or of the *realms of meaning*.   Hence, a philosophy of the curriculum requires a mapping of the realms of meaning, one in which the various possibilities of significant experience are charted and the various domains of meaning are distinguished and correlated.

Six fundamental patterns of meaning emerge from the analysis of the possible distinctive modes of human understanding.   These six patterns may be designated respectively as *symbolics, empirics, esthetics, synnoetics, ethics,* and *synoptics.*

Each realm of meaning and each of its constituent subrealms may be described by reference to its typical methods, leading ideas, and characteristic structures.   These features may be exhibited both in their uniqueness for each realm or subrealm and in their relationships and continuities with the other types of meaning.   Leaving the details to be elaborated in subsequent chapters, the six realms can be broadly characterized as follows:

The first realm, *symbolics,* comprises ordinary language, mathematics, and various types of nondiscursive symbolic forms, such as gestures, rituals, rhythmic patterns, and the like.   These meanings are contained in arbitrary symbolic structures, with socially accepted rules of formation and transformation, created as instruments for the expression and communication of any meaning whatsoever.   These symbolic systems in one respect constitute the most fundamental of all the realms of meaning in that they must be employed to express the meanings in each of the other realms.

The second realm, *empirics,* includes the sciences of the physical world, of living things, and of man.   These sciences provide factual descriptions, generalizations, and theoretical formulations and explanations which are based upon observation and experimentation in the world of matter, life, mind, and society.   They express meanings as probable empirical truths framed in accordance with certain rules of evidence and verification and making use of specified systems of analytic abstraction.

The third realm, *esthetics,* contains the various arts, such as music, the visual arts, the arts of movement, and literature.

Meanings in this realm are concerned with the contemplative perception of particular significant things as unique objectifications of ideated subjectivities.

The fourth realm, *synnoetics*, embraces what Michael Polanyi calls "personal knowledge" and Martin Buber the "I-Thou" relation. The novel term "synnoetics," which was devised because no existing concept appeared adequate to the type of understanding intended, derives from the Greek *synnoesis*, meaning "meditative thought," and thus in turn is compounded of *syn*, meaning "with" or "together," and *noesis*, meaning "cognition." Thus synnoetics signifies "relational insight" or "direct awareness." It is analogous in the sphere of knowing to sympathy in the sphere of feeling. This personal or relational knowledge is concrete, direct, and existential. It may apply to other persons, to oneself, or even to things.

The fifth realm, *ethics*, includes moral meanings that express obligation rather than fact, perceptual form, or awareness of relation. In contrast to the sciences, which are concerned with abstract cognitive understanding, to the arts, which express idealized esthetic perceptions, and to personal knowledge, which reflects intersubjective understanding, morality has to do with personal conduct that is based on free, responsible, deliberate decision.

The sixth realm, *synoptics*, refers to meanings that are comprehensively integrative. It includes history, religion, and philosophy. These disciplines combine empirical, esthetic, and synnoetic meanings into coherent wholes. Historical interpretation comprises an artful re-creation of the past, in obedience to factual evidence, for the purpose of revealing what man by his deliberate choices has made of himself within the context of his given circumstances. Religion is concerned with ultimate meanings, that is, with meanings from any realm whatsoever, considered from the standpoint of such boundary concepts as the Whole, the Comprehensive, and the Transcendent. Philosophy provides analytic clarification, evaluation, and synthetic coordination of all the other realms through a reflective conceptual interpretation of all possible kinds of meaning in their distinctiveness and in their interrelationships.

The symbolics, which have been placed at one end of the spectrum of meanings, encompass the entire range of meanings because they are the necessary means of expressing all meanings whatever. Similarly, the synoptics, which have been placed at the other end of the spectrum, also gather up the entire range of meanings by virtue of their integrative character. Between these two realms of symbolics and synoptics lie the realms of empirics, esthetics, synnoetics, and ethics as four essentially distinct (though interdependent) dimensions of meaning or modes of significant human relatedness to the world and to existence.

The six realms thus charted provide the foundations for all the meanings that enter into human experience. They are the foundations in the sense that they are the pure and archetypal kinds of meaning that determine the quality of every humanly significant experience. From this viewpoint, any particular meaning can be analyzed as an expression of one of the fundamental meanings or as a combination of two or more of them. In practice, meanings seldom appear in pure and simple form; they are almost always compounded of several of the elemental types.

Despite this complexity in practice, it is useful for purposes of curriculum analysis and construction to distinguish the basic ingredients in all meaning and to order the learning process for general education in the light of these elements.

If the six realms cover the range of possible meanings, they may be regarded as comprising the basic competences that general education should develop in every person. A complete person should be skilled in the use of speech, symbol, and gesture, factually well informed, capable of creating and appreciating objects of esthetic significance, endowed with a rich and disciplined life in relation to self and others, able to make wise decisions and to judge between right and wrong, and possessed of an integral outlook. These are the aims of general education for the development of whole persons.

* * * * * * * * *

Philip Phenix
(1966)

[From *Education and the Worship of God* (Philadelphia: The Westminster Press, 1966), pp. 163-76.]

In the foregoing chapters we have explored the religious dimensions in five fields of disciplined scholarship. It remains now to draw the various strands together into a synoptic view of the relevance of faith to the curriculum of the school and to consider how this perspective can become effective in educational practice.

Our theme throughout has been that religion consists in "practicing the presence of God," to use the familiar phrase of Brother Lawrence. Since faith is one's total life commitment, it manifests itself in everything one does. The worship and service of God are not limited to conventionally holy occasions but take place chiefly in the conduct of apparently secular affairs, including those of teaching and learning. In particular, the organized disciplines of the school curriculum afford especially abundant opportunities to grow in the knowledge of truth and righteousness and thus to respond more faithfully to the divine persuasion.

From the standpoint of faith, each discipline reveals different aspects of ultimate reality and evokes a distinctive set of reverential responses. The study of language primarily discloses the God who speaks. The ultimately real is seen, not as a collection of isolated, self-contained entities, but as an intercommunicating network of beings. The fact of language is of fundamental importance for understanding the profound truth that the striving for mutuality and relation, strikingly exemplified in human speech, is deeply rooted in the nature of things.

The study of science reveals the God who knows. The ultimately real is seen, not as a random assortment of things, but at least to some degree as an intelligible order. The success of the scientific enterprise is evidence that mind is not alien to nature, and that the drive for the rational ordering of experience is grounded in the structures of existence itself.

The study of the arts manifests the God who makes. The ultimately real is seen not only as a world of things that are but also as an infinite treasure of realizable possibilities inviting individual embodiment. The perennial appeal of the various arts bears witness to the primordial significance of singular concretions and of the creative process in which human beings may deliberately participate.

The study of ethics shows forth the God who judges. The ultimately real is seen, not simply as an array of neutral existents, but as a matrix of values. The experiences of moral deliberation and responsible choice support the affirmation of an order of obligation rooted not merely in personal preference or social convenience, but in a personal ground of being intimated in the leadings of conscience.

The study of history yields knowledge of the God who plans. The ultimately real is seen, not as a series of independent accidental happenings, but as a fabric of events that fulfill a significant world destiny. Each occurrence is influenced by its inheritance from the past and in turn contributes to the future so as to realize eternal purposes that are at least partially discerned in the major world-transforming events and movements of the historical tradition.

Study and teaching in each discipline, in depth, thus constitute *de facto* acts of religious devotion, even though conventional religious symbols and concepts may not be employed. At the same time, traditional theological ideas may provide valuable assistance in making explicit the potential ultimacies in educational pursuits, and the religious ideas may in turn be clarified, corrected, and vivified by relating them to the interpretation of experience through the academic disciplines.

Each discipline affords only certain perspectives on what is supremely true and excellent. No one line of study can be expected to yield a full and adequate vision of God. The whole truth includes insights that embrace all the deepest revelations of speech, knowledge, construction, judgment, and purpose--and more. The channel of full religious devotion cannot be only Word, or Wisdom, or Work, or Will, or Way. All are required for the complete devotion that is fitting in the worship of the one God.

Since God in any case is one and indivisible, the disclosures of the divine mysteries in language, science, art, ethics, history, and other studies in the last analysis cannot be independent and separate. Word, Wisdom, Work, Will, and

Way represent interdependent aspects of the one ultimate reality. These interrelations are evident even at the penultimate level. Language is a necessary means of expression in every other discipline. No field of study can succeed without the aid of the empirical knowledge systematically developed in scientific investigation. Every study, and not only the arts, has creative and constructive aspects. No human pursuit--not even the most rigorously objective scientific research--is independent of ethical considerations. Finally, every activity of inquiry is an outgrowth of historical development and in turn contributes to the current making of history. These interconnections in the context of finitude are confirmed in the context of infinitude. For example, the God revealed in the ultimacies of speaking is also the primordial source of knowledge. The God disclosed in the ultimacies of perceptual construction is also the source of moral authority. When God speaks, knows, makes, and judges, he thereby unfolds his plan in the history of which he is Lord.

By means of the various disciplines in the curriculum, corresponding human abilities are developed. When these studies are pursued with religious insight and commitment, the realization of the divine nature in human persons is fostered. People grow in conformity to what they love. The worship of God tends to transform the worshiper into the likeness of God. thus, as the student in reverence and devotion acquires the powers of speaking, knowing, making, judging, and planning, he becomes increasingly an exemplar of the divine nature. By the same token, the personal qualities of those who most profoundly realize the potentialities in human existence are clues to the nature of God.

The practice of the presence of God throughout the school curriculum will flourish only in a general spiritual context that is hospitable to the type of religious outlook recommended in the preceding pages. The worship of God cannot occur naturally in the regular course of study unless certain conditions prevail in the cultural temper and attitude. These conditions are requisite to the development of religious depth in general education. The following are some of the main ingredients in such a hospitable spiritual situation.

One ingredient is the affirmation of life and the world. In a climate of pessimism about the values and the possibilities of the human enterprise people do not look for the deeper significance of civilized pursuits. They do no more than make the best of a fundamentally unsatisfactory predicament. Expecting the worst, they ask no questions beyond those necessary to navigate with maximum speed and safety through the dangerous waters of existence. The spirit of worship, on the other hand, stems from a fundamental optimism. This is not a superficial cheerfulness sustained by systematic avoidance of the evil and the ugly. It is a confidence that life is good despite all suffering, loss, and frustration.

This persuasion of the worth of life is an elemental endowment. It is not a conclusion derived from a local argument, but a premise from which all conclusions must be derived. It is not a consequence of faith, but faith's very root and ground. It is not the result of ultimate concern, but the energy animating such concern. This positive outlook on existence is a gift of grace from the fountainhead of being. It cannot be generated by an act of will or by the processes of thought, for will and thought are themselves derivative from it.

People will care and dare enough to teach and learn in depth only if they have a profound intuition of the goodness of life. An age dominated by skepticism and cynicism is not favorable to the exploration of ultimate meanings, for such probing will be expected to yield only deeper doubts and confusions. The destructive conflicts of the present century have led multitudes to question the viability of the whole civilized endeavor, and to doubt that any proximate, let alone ultimate, values can be manifest in it. At the same time, the conflicts themselves are a kind of perverse evidence of passionate belief in life; people do not accept the actualities of their existence in passive acquiescence. Perhaps the now ever present consciousness of the possibility of annihilation through nuclear warfare will stimulate a fresh and abiding awareness of the preciousness of life and strengthen the determination to save civilization from extinction. It may be that the time is ripe for a fundamental reaffirmation of the

possibilities of life and hence for new adventures in faith
through the exploration of the religious dimensions in every
field of learning.

Implicit in the affirmative spirit is the conviction that the
way to the fulfillment of existence lies in continued inquiry
and invention, using the powers of human reason and
imagination, and not in retreat to a simpler age or
renunciation of this world in favor of another. This is not to
deny that human intelligence and creativity can be and often
are employed for evil purposes, thus dishonoring God and
tarnishing his image in man. Nevertheless, the cure for this
perversion of abilities does not consist in rejecting the
civilized enterprise and the education that sustains it, but in
thinking still more profoundly and acting still more resolutely
in the faith that the pursuit of knowledge and skill will in the
end yield the peaceable fruits of righteousness.

A second element in a spiritual atmosphere favorable to
practicing the divine presence in education is general concern
for the relevance of faith to the affairs of everyday life.
People for whom religion is a special kind of experience
associated with special times, places, and events do not want
it contaminated by contact with business, politics, family life,
recreation, and education. They want their religion straight
and not mixed with worldly ingredients. If it is introduced
into education, they want to practice it according to the
familiar forms of explicit worship and not as a dimension
implicit in secular studies. Such people recognize God as
present in holy events only by virtue of their outward
contrast with profane events, in which he is regarded as
absent. The practice of the divine omnipresence presupposes
a completely different orientation in which faith is regarded
as a total commitment of life, manifest in everything that one
does. Religion is conceived as the animating and directing
principle in culture, including the activities of education.
Within such an orientation, people judge the character of a
person's religion less by his affiliation and his creed than by
the quality of his choices and the objects of his greatest
interest and affection.

Despite the emphasis of religious leaders on the relevance
of religion to all of life, the special, compartmental
conception still widely prevails, probably because such
fencing off is a protection against the disturbing visions and

transforming judgments of a relevant faith. Nevertheless, there are also signs that the larger conception of religion is gaining ground. Leading thinkers like Paul Tillich, Jacques Maritain, and Martin Buber are creating an influential theology of culture that may eventually win general acceptance among informed people for the broader view of religion. When the idea of faith as comprehensive life orientation and of religious dimensions as ultimate perspectives in any domain of human experience becomes widely accepted, the way will be open for the worship of God in the regular subjects of the school curriculum.

A third component in a cultural context favorable to a fundamentally religious approach to education is the ecumenical spirit. Perhaps the most serious obstacle to dealing with the religious dimensions in education is the sectarian spirit. When organized religions insist on the exclusive correctness of their doctrines and practices, it becomes necessary, in a society with many different religious groups, to avoid explicit references to religion in public education for the sake of peace and order. Each group objects to attempts by nonmembers to represent its position, and it regards with disfavor instruction concerning what it holds to be the erroneous views of other groups. As a result, students are deprived not only of knowledge about the historic faiths but also of the illumination of ultimate meanings afforded by the religious traditions of mankind. Moreover, sectarianism stands in the way of an interpretation of religion as comprehensive life orientation, since so much attention must be paid to the propagation and defense of explicit religious forms.

The ecumenical spirit results from the acceptance of human finitude and fallibility in matters of belief and conduct and from the recognition that people with different endowments and diverse histories may usefully complement each other in the pursuit of truth and righteousness. Ecumenicity is based finally on acknowledgment of the divine omnipresence. God is not the possession of any one group or tradition. He is the deepest reality and the highest value for all people, and as such, every person, without exception, meets him in every moment of life, regardless of any explicit recognition of that meeting. Furthermore, it is the one true God who is thus encountered and not the God whom one acknowledges and worships in his particular sect. Because man is finite and fallible, the God he claims to know and serve is not likely to be in all respects the one true God. It follows that no person or group is justified in claiming complete understanding of God or exclusive channels of access to him.

The humility and openness of the ecumenical attitude do not, however, preclude firm convictions and commitments. Nor does this attitude entail the acceptance of all faiths as equally valid. Since a genuine religious commitment reflects what one really believes to be universally true and right, it is incompatible with belief in the equal validity of all other faiths. Nevertheless, such commitment is not incompatible with acknowledging the unperceived limitations of one's own perspective, with a concern to discover what other people believe and why, and with a readiness to modify one's own concepts and actions in the light of new experience.

The consequence of ecumenicity is thus neither uniformity nor indifference, but a continuing dialogue. Differences in faith and practice continue, but no longer as mutually exclusive, hostile, sectarian systems. People are open to fresh insights on the basis of working and conversing together and particularly through finding opportunities for common worship.

Ecumenism is one of the outstanding phenomena of organized religion in the twentieth century. Religious bodies are faced with the realities of worldwide interdependence and with abundant evidence of the disastrous consequences of intergroup conflict. They are also confronted with the challenge of vigorous new secular faiths that present impressive alternatives to traditional religious affiliation. Consequently, sustained attempts are being made by religious groups to discover bases for cooperation and mutual reinforcement. While the earliest and most successful of these efforts were made by the various Protestant groups, impressive gains toward mutual understanding are now being achieved among Roman Catholics and Eastern Orthodox and Protestants. Jews and Christians are establishing better relations, and interfaith conversations are even taking place with Islam and with Hinduism and Buddhism.

The logical conclusion of ecumenical activity is to extend the dialogue beyond the bounds of the traditional organized religions to include those who do not call themselves religious, but who are nevertheless deeply committed to knowing the truth and serving the supreme good. From such interchanges may come new insights into the ultimate commitments shared by sincere worshipers in both the "sacred" and "secular" traditions. This full ecumenicity also provides the context most favorable to the worship of God in education through discerning the religious dimensions in every area of the curriculum.

A fourth factor favorable to the worship of God in the apparently secular concerns of education is the general acceptance of lay initiative in religious affairs. The compartmentalizing of life into sacred and secular spheres is abetted by making a sharp distinction between the religious functions of clergy and laity. With such a dualism, the clergy are regarded as the principal or exclusive guardians and dispensers of religion, and laymen are expected to manage secular affairs. The priests maintain the security and purity of the sacred inheritance, and the lay people are responsible for ministering to the worldly needs of men. The holy men have charge of holy things and the common men deal with common things. In the sphere of education, a corresponding division is made between sacred studies, conducted by authorized religious teachers, and secular studies, conducted by lay teachers.

This neat division of responsibility is not compatible with a serious acceptance of the divine omnipresence. Even though religious organizations may appropriately appoint people to special offices for the more efficient conduct of the communal life, no one can be religious for another. Every person has to make his own commitment of life and arrive at his own convictions about what is ultimately true and supremely important. Faith is each person's own unique responsibility, which can never be delegated to anyone else. Hence the division between clergy and laity is at most one of office and social function within institutional religion. In the presence of God the distinction between priest and layman vanishes, and all are invited, in the full inwardness of their being, to dedicate themselves to divine worship and service through all the occupations in which they are engaged, whether ostensibly sacred or secular.

Vital and relevant religion depends on widespread lay concern about matters of faith.   Dominant clericalism destroys the connection between religion--and life and leads to stagnation and sterility in organized religion.   At the present time a renewed sense of lay responsibility is clearly evident.   It is becoming widely acknowledged that the ultimate meaning of life is not to be discovered and interpreted only by professional theologians and religious officials, but also by artists, scientists, politicians, businessmen, educators, and other lay people in every walk of life. The time is therefore at hand for the assumption of responsibility by lay teachers in all disciplines for helping to make clear the religious dimensions in the regular studies of the curriculum.

A fifth condition favorable to practicing the presence of God in education is an open society committed to religious liberty. Worship by its very nature is an act of free devotion. It cannot be coerced.   Consequently, when religious observances are required by law or supervised by political agencies, they are transformed into civic rites and tend to lose their sacred quality.   The Constitutional prohibition of religious establishment and of any laws limiting the free exercise of religion was adopted by the American Founding Fathers in recognition of the fact that government cannot properly be the arbiter of ultimate commitments. Matters of faith and conscience lie outside the province of political regulation.   Sovereignty belongs, not to the political order, but only to God from whom alone the state and all its agencies derive their existence and their true authority.

From the principle of religious liberty it follows that the public school, which is an agency of the civil government, may not assume the role of a religious organization by indoctrinating the students in the beliefs and ceremonies of any religion. By the same principle, the public school should not in the name of neutrality and objectivity exclude traditional religious elements and ultimate concerns from the curriculum, thereby effectively abridging the freedom to worship as both conscience and the subject matter invite one to do.   The free society is not, as those who urge the exclusion of all religious elements from public education suppose, one in which religion is banished altogether from public affairs. In such a society doctrinaire secularism is in effect the established religion, and the exercise of other religions is seriously inhibited. In a free society the citizens are given every possible opportunity to worship according to the leadings of their conscience, subject only to the proviso that the religious liberty of other persons is not infringed.

In public schools where several faiths are represented, traditional forms of devotion cannot be used for common worship without such infringement. However, other forms of religious expression that do not presuppose a common tradition orientation are appropriate. In particular, in a free society it is not only fitting but academically requisite that students be encouraged to pursue their regular studies in a reverential manner and with due awareness of the religious dimensions in the various disciplines. Furthermore, ample provision should be made in all schools for the informed consideration of the many traditional religious symbols by means of which the ultimate significance of studies can be illuminated. This kind of religiously oriented scholarship can be carried on in dialogue, with complete freedom for each person to respond according to his deepest intellectual and moral insights.

A sixth ingredient in a situation favorable to practicing the divine presence in education is academic freedom, which is the educational counterpart of religious liberty. Just as faith is a sham apart from free commitment, so convictions about truth and excellence are hypocritical apart from freedom to inquire. When teachers are prevented from handling their subject matter in the light of the best available evidence because of prior determinations about admissible methods or conclusions, the most fundamental principle of academic ethics is denied. Even when beliefs acquired under constraint are abstractly true, they are personally fraudulent, because they do not derive from a free personal response to the truth.

Academic freedom does not mean, of course, that the teacher is at liberty to teach whatever he pleases. It means only that his teaching is not to be determined by requirements that are incompatible with the professional understanding of the teacher. Here the qualifier "professional" is important. Academic freedom is no excuse for incompetence. It presupposes responsible teachers who know their subject and are able to give good reasons for what they teach. They are not at liberty to teach what lies outside of their sphere of academic competence. The principle of academic freedom excludes only restraints operating against the full exercise of reason, skill, and evaluative judgment within the domain of competence in which the teacher has been appointed to serve.

This linking of freedom with competence in the field of appointment may be used as the basis for arguing that teachers of "secular" subjects should not be at liberty to introduce religious matters into their teaching, both because they were not hired to teach religion and because they are not trained to teach it. This argument is sound only if "religion" is understood as a separate domain and not as a dimension that pertains to every subject of study. If the term "religion" is used in the sense of comprehensive life orientation, then one who teaches a "secular" subject with due regard to its sacred perspectives does not thereby transgress into subject fields to which he was not assigned or deal with matters outside of his proper area of professional concern, since the religious dimensions are inherent in the academic pursuit itself, when conducted with sincere devotion.

From this point of view, the worship of God in the teaching and study of "secular" subjects need not constitute an irresponsible abuse of academic freedom. It would be irresponsible for the teacher to use the classroom as a place for propagating a particular faith by injecting religious ideas into the study materials other than as required by the nature of the subject matter itself. On the other hand, teaching with concern for ultimate meanings exemplifies academic responsibility of the highest order. Reverence in the pursuit of truth and excellence is, in fact, the quintessence of responsibility in any discipline. Academic freedom is itself a religious ideal. It is based on the presupposition that no human being is an infallible authority concerning truth and righteousness and hence that no humanly imposed limitations on the disciplined pursuit of excellence are justified. Such limitations negate the religious dimensions of scholarship by enclosing it within finite bounds, thus denying that openness to the infinite mysteries of being which is the essential condition for reverence.

Academic freedom is today widely cherished and jealously guarded. Scholars and teachers, together with the many in other callings who are aware of how largely the advancement of learning, and of civilization generally, depends upon full inquiry, are determined that the discovery and dissemination of knowledge shall not be subject to extrinsic controls, whether ecclesiastical, political, or economic. One of the most effective ways of practicing this freedom and of making its reality evident is to engage in each discipline of study with the unconditional openness and the bold rejection of all arbitrary limitations that are characteristic of religious orientation.

Another factor in the general outlook that is relevant to religious concerns in the curriculum has to do with the concepts of neutrality and objectivity in the academic enterprise. A common assumption among people reared in the traditions of modern science and positivistic philosophy is that true knowledge is value free, and therefore that the scholar or teacher ought to be neutral with respect to values. His only concern should be to discover and communicate what is objectively true, without regard to his own preferences or commitments. Since religion manifestly rests upon personal dedication, it follows from the neutralist point of view that religious considerations have no place in education. Within the positivist framework this conclusion holds for education under any auspices, public or private, since the truth is the same for all and can be acquired only under conditions of impersonality and detachment.

The more sophisticated contemporary analyses of the ways of knowing show that this positivistic dogma is not tenable. It is now acknowledged by many students of the methodology of inquiry that all human activities, including those of critical scholarship, manifest certain human interests and presuppose certain values. As a purposive agent, everything a person does expresses his governing commitments. Accordingly, the idea of absolute neutrality is inapplicable to any human affairs, including those of teaching and learning. Such a concept is incompatible with the very meaning of being a living, deciding person.

Of course, a concept of relative neutrality is admissible. It is an appropriate principle of scholarship to examine different points of view and not to come to conclusions prematurely, without considering the arguments from a variety of perspectives. It is also fitting that personal preconceptions and preferences be tested by methods of intersubjective analysis and criticism. But these methodological principles themselves are manifestations of certain fundamental commitments. Their purpose is to ensure that truth rather than error shall be served and that knowledge shall be a shared and not merely a private benefit. The detachment and objectivity appropriate to the scholar are not absolute. They apply only in relation to the particular involvements that cause distortion of view.

Contemporary investigations of the knowing process underscore the human interests that motivate even the most objective and critical inquiries, for objectivity and criticism are themselves goals preferred to other possibilities and passionately striven for. From this standpoint it is not possible to maintain full neutrality as an academic ideal and thus to exclude considerations of faith from education. On the contrary, it is now evident that questions of ultimate commitment are implicit in the very principles of scholarship itself, in its various kinds. Thus one is led to affirm the basic importance of the religious dimensions in all the disciplines of the curriculum.

Finally, the practice of worship in education is fostered within a cultural context of general concern for qualitative excellence. The religious dimensions are submerged in times when education is conceived purely as a means of transmitting a received tradition or of gaining economic and social mobility. Under such conditions teaching and learning have utilitarian purposes and serve only finite practical ends; sacred concerns are submerged under a tide of secular activity. The religious element comes to the fore when people are able to transcend considerations of acquisition, whether of a tradition or of things, and turn their attention to the pursuit of excellence. The primary concern then is not with quantity and position, but with value and significance.

The success of advanced technical societies in solving the material problems of existence is leading to larger concern for the qualitative meanings of life. Education is now not looked to only for social and occupational competence but also for significant purposes and visions of nobility. Liberal learning has always had this larger goal, but it has not until recently been conceived as perhaps the most important objective of universal general education. From this standpoint, schools are not established mainly to prepare people to make a good living, but to live a good life.

Once this general qualitative concern is established, the consideration of religious issues follows naturally, for these have to do with what the good life really is and what is worthy of one's highest devotion. The way is thus open for dealing with the fundamental values that can be realized through the dedicated study of the various academic disciplines.

Recent Developments

JED and Princeton's M.A. Syllabus

The late 1960's through the early 1980's in American Protestant mainline religious education could be characterized only as ecletically diverse. While liberation theology was catching the imaginations of many leaders in religious education, neo-orthodoxy remained the norm for others. Educational models used were equally diverse and equally eclectic. Two representative samples from this period are the stance paper of Joint Educational Development (JED), and Princeton Theological Seminary's syllabus for the professional exam leading to the Master of Arts in Christian Education.

JED was the most significant ecumenical event in Protestant mainline religious education of the 1970's. The Christian Church (Disciples of Christ), Church of the Brethren, Cumberland Presbyterian Church, Episcopal Church, Evangelical Covenant Church, Moravian Church in America, Moravian Church, Southern Province, Presbyterian Church in Canada, Presbyterian Church in the U.S., Reformed Church in America, United Church of Canada, United Church of Christ, and United Presbyterian Church in the USA were all guided in their national educational goals by the JED stance paper.

The Princeton Theological Seminary M.A. syllabus, given original form and direction by Wyckoff, went through many revisions through the years. Its clear theological focus, and its educational claims, however, remained constant. It stands as a classic formulation of the relationship between education and theology.

* * * * * * * * * *

"A Stance Toward the Future:
Where We Are--Where We Hope To Go"

[From *Doing Church Education Together: Why and How JED Works* (Atlanta: Joint Educational Development, 1978), pp. 5-12.]

PREFACE: THE JED PROCESS

The "jed" process of joint educational development began in 1967 when national educational staffs of the Episcopal Church, The United Church of Christ, and the United Presbyterian Church in the USA appointed a task force to outline a rational planning strategy for joint efforts. Step one of this strategy was an attempt to look at the society and culture in which the church may well be set during the next two decades. The task force exploring the culture attempted to delineate major issues or problems that will face American society in the decade of the 70's.

A year later the Joint Educational Development planners, by now including the Presbyterian Church in the U.S., reviewed and basically affirmed the work of the task force on societal issues. Further steps in the planning strategy were then set in motion by the appointment of task forces to deal with: (1) the shape of the church in the 70's; (2) the shape of general education in the years ahead; and (3) the shape of church education in the 70' and 80's. These task forces submitted their findings in the Fall of 1969. By that time, the Reformed Church in America and the Christian Churches (Disciples of Christ) had come into JED. Their staffs then joined with the others in the process of discovering interrelationships and implications in the findings of the separate task forces. That task is by no means complete. It never will be because we consider JED to be an ongoing process, not a completed project or an organizational structure. In January 1970, the work of the task forces of the JED Coordinating Committee, and of the Committee of

Executives of the cooperating denominational agencies was
reviewed by a representative group of national staff members,
Board members, and seminary personnel. A paper indicating
our basic stance for joint educational development was
authorized. That stance paper has been used and revised and
attempts to describe the positions at which JED has thus far
arrived, in light of which we work in joint educational
development.

A STANCE TOWARD THE FUTURE

Our Christian faith affirms that God is Lord of history.
God, who has acted for the salvation of the world in the
past--supremely in Jesus Christ--is God of the future. This
affirmation undergirds the present work of Joint Educational
Development and its stance toward the future. Those
involved in the JED partnership proceed in the faith that God
is acting in our time: creating, judging, liberating, and
redeeming the whole human community; renewing and
reforming the church of Jesus Christ; and calling God's
people to faithfulness in mission. A significant part of that
mission is expressed in educational ministry.

As participants in JED, it is our intention to develop and
implement educational ministries that will be faithful to the
gospel and relevant to the lives of people. Under the
guidance of the Holy Spirit and using the best of human
wisdom, we in JED will seek to make our educational
ministries an expression of our unity in Jesus Christ and a
means for effectively carrying on the mission in the church
and in the world.

The impetus for this joint planning and educational ministry
comes from two sources. It comes, first, from the Christian
claim that God is at work in the world and calls the church to
serve the world: the "push" of the gospel. Second, it comes
from the concrete situation of people, individually and
corporately: the "pull of the world."

Agenda for Educational Ministry
in the Christian Community

This dual impetus--the gospel and the concrete situation of people in today's world--provides the basic agenda for the church's educational ministry. The church is called to tell the story of the faith in such a way that it intersects with people's lives and with the personal and social issues that confront the human community. The basic agenda includes, therefore, the story of faith, the faith community, and the human situation.

1. *The story of faith.* The biblical witness to God's action in the world, with its climax in the life, ministry, death, and resurrection of Jesus of Nazareth, is the essential witness the church must make in every generation. This story of God;s deeds provides the faith perspective from which we, as Christians, discern God's continuing mission in the world.

The biblical story is the foundation of the faith story, but the latter includes the witness of Christians of different racial, national, and cultural traditions to what God has done within their particular histories. In today's world, we are called to give special attention to these different histories --to claim them and share them with one another that they may become different strands within the one story that belongs to all members of the worldwide Christian community.

The faith story must be both claimed and proclaimed. In making our proclamation, however, the Christian community recognizes that we are not the source of the gospel or of the meaning system the gospel provides. Rather, we must continually examine and re-examine the unfinished story of God's action in the world, seeking fuller understanding of that story. The church's proclamation of the story must always point beyond itself to the continuing activity of the God who loves all persons and judges all human activity, including that of the church. This means that the church avoids enshrining current understandings and expressions of the gospel. Today, and in the future, the Christian community must pay particular attention to the pluralistic character of our world and seek to engage in open dialogue with as many alternative meaning systems as possible. In such dialogue the church will avoid making pretentious claims to the absolute validity of its own perceptions of what God is doing in the world. Our claims as Christians are confessional and subject to the power of the gospel to correct our perceptions.

2. *The faith community.* The faith community is responsible for telling the faith story. This community in all its forms is marked by its proclamation that Jesus Christ is Lord; its recognition of the Bible as the source of its faith perspective, doctrine, and practice; and its view of the sacraments as means of grace. The church, in all its manifestations, is self-consciously rooted in and linked with the historic and universal church. The institutional life of the church is essential to maintain this linkage, but no one institutional form is to be considered normative. In today's world it is especially important that the church be open to new forms and to new movements of the Holy Spirit within it.

3. *The situation of people in today's world.* If the faith story is to intersect with The real-life situations of people, the church must be in the midst of, and responsive to, those situations. All persons face the human experiences of loneliness, community, joy, meaninglessness, fulfillment, alienation. All of us face the fact of death and the reality of human sinfulness. Social forces push and pull at people, often oppressing, dehumanizing, depersonalizing, and imprisoning them. In the interplay of these social forces with human sin, injustice in society is perpetuated and community is destroyed. The increasing complexity and interdependence of our world, while binding the whole of humanity together, also separates, as the magnitude of our social system allows entrenched injustice to become more deeply rooted and institutionalized. To create and sustain social forces that will correct systemic injustice and move toward a more humane world requires not only personal responsibility, but also long-range, intelligent, purposeful, corporate action in society.

We believe that the faith story enables us to look into the depths of our human situation in both its personal and social dimensions. Our faith story also provides perspectives from which we may discern what God, in our time, is doing among people and nations. Through that story we know we are called to prophetic servanthood in God's mission.

A major part of the faith community's agenda, especially in its educational ministry, is, therefore, to equip its own membership with the story and with the skills required to discern and participate in God's mission. But the church's responsibility goes beyond its own membership as its witness moves into the community, nation and world. The Christian community today is especially called to seek out those who are concerned for a just and humane society and have a vision of world community, and to join forces for effective action. As Christians we bring the critique of our own faith perspectives to all that we do, but we cannot claim that we alone are God's instruments in the world.

How congregations and other church bodies perform their ministry and mission depends upon many factors. Among them are the congregation's own understanding of its mission to its members and to the world, the nature of its membership, and its relationship to its own community and to the wider world; and the quantity and quality of the programs it can offer.

Intentions of Educational Ministry

The church's educational ministry encompasses the planned educational programs of the church and the educational influence of its total life and mission. The whole ministry needs to be intentionally planned in such a way that it has purpose and direction. Within the JED partnership the present understanding of the direction and purpose of educational ministry is outlined in the following four intentions:

1.   The Christian community engages in education as a continuing means of sharing the gospel and of helping persons to make their own responses of faith; to broaden and deepen their perceptions of God, other persons, social issues and structures, and the natural world; and to develop skills of ethical decision-making and responsible participation in shaping the future of the human community.

2.   The Christian community engages in education as a means of equipping persons to understand, to enter into, and to help develop the life and ministries of a contemporary community of faith, rooted in the Christian heritage and charged with mission.

3.   The Christian community engages in education as a means for helping persons to achieve the full human stature that we believe God intends. This involves:

a. a sense of personal dignity, capacity, and
worth;
b. interpersonal relationships of trust, freedom,
and love;
c. global society that enhances freedom,
justice, and peace for all people.

4.   The Christian community engages in education as a
means of effecting justice and reconciliation within and
through all social structures and systems.   Essential to
accomplishing this intention is an understanding of the
interdependence of all people and a willingness to act to
change the present unjust distribution of power and economic
resources in the world.

Theological and Educational Stance

The following are affirmations about the educational and
theological stance of our educational ministry. We believe
that they are fundamental to planning and carrying out
education in the church. The affirmations are interdependent
and no attempt has made to weight them in relation to one
another. This list cannot comprehend all the elements that
will come into play as the JED process continues. It does,
however, constitute our present estimate of the stance that
gives most promise of effectiveness in educational ministry in
the years just ahead.

1. *We affirm that the educational ministries of the church
must be ecumenical in both context and thrust.* Educational
planning   should   be   collaborative   and   as   broadly
interdenominational as possible at every point of planning--
local, national, regional.   Educational planning is currently
closest among the denominations participating in JED, but
ongoing planning and development will attempt to be open to
as wide a segment of the Christian community as possible.

We see our commitment as ecumenical in a more
fundamental sense.   The Christian community is concerned
with the *oikumene* of God--the whole inhabited earth, which
is the scene of God's action.   This ecumenical thrust means
that God's whole world and all its people are both context
and content of educational ministry.

2. *We affirm that educational ministries should be characterized by racial, ethnic, and socioeconomic inclusiveness.* To the extent that such inclusiveness is not achieved, the quality of education is impaired. Deliberate provision for the interaction of persons of various races, ethnic groups, and socioeconomic classes is essential. Also essential is the sharing of one another's stories and cultural traditions in order that we may know the fullness of God's work among us. Such inclusiveness will not aim to homogenize persons of various backgrounds. Instead, it will seek to provide occasions for all persons to affirm their integrity, distinctiveness; and value.

We are painfully aware that this commitment constitutes a severe judgment upon, and challenge to, the JED participants because of the socioeconomic and racial compositions of the denominations and churches involved.

3. *We affirm a biblical and theological rootage and style.* Throughout our planning and in the educational processes and programs we may devise or advocate, we find our impetus in our faith story--in the good news of God's past and continuing action in human life, mediated to us through the scriptures and uniquely in the person of Jesus of Nazareth. We also affirm that active theological reflection is imperative in order to develop a continually growing and deepening Christian perspective on the meaning of faith and life as it is lived out in given moments in history. Such a rootage and style demand serious attention to the biblical and historical heritage that informs contemporary reflections on the Christian faith.

4. *We affirm that the faith community is itself part of God's mission.* Its own life must, therefore, be continually nurtured and strengthened. Although institutional maintenance is never an end in itself, a strong institutional base must be maintained if the Christian community is to have continuity and strength in mission. A significant part of the educational task is that of drawing persons into the community of faith, initiating them into the heritage, the ethos, and the values of the community, and providing opportunities for their full participation in shaping its life. Another significant educational task is that of equipping the membership of the Christian community for leadership responsibilities in its life and mission.

5. *We affirm that valid education and authentic worship are interrelated.* Worship includes elements of celebration and awe in response to God's goodness, judgment, power, and mystery. In it we reenact the story of what God has done among us, using the richness of our Christian heritage, significant art forms, and different cultural expressions.

6. *We affirm that educational ministry is concerned for the total person as a thinking, acting, feeling being--a complexly organized self-in-world who acts upon his or her environment as well as being acted upon by it.* Education must deal with persons in their wholeness. In addition to enabling persons to think and to know, educational ministry also enables persons to feel and to experience the realities of the Christian faith and of the human situation. Education must reflect the cognitive, emotive, and experiential aspects of human learning and do this in the context of the person's developmental level, life situation, and human relationships. Within this context, the person must be dealt with as an active participant in his or her own learning as a shaper of meanings and values and a creater of his or her own story.

7. *We affirm an open-ended and dialogic approach.* Because God is continually at work, education in the Christian community ought to be open to ever new perceptions of God's action. Because people must do their own learning and thinking, educational processes ought to encourage learners to engage in their own inquiries and pursue their own questions. Honest dialogue with divergent points of view should be encouraged within a climate of willingness to re-examine current perspectives on the meaning of Christian faith, the functioning of society, and the meaning and role of personal life. Arriving at predetermined conclusions should not be made the measure of success in education. Rather, an open-ended approach that encourages inquiry should characterize teaching and learning.

8. *We affirm both action and reflection as intrinsic to education.* The educational process should engage persons in action as well as study, reflection, and analysis. The process can begin from either action or reflection. Both points of initiation are part of a continuum that requires both to be present.

9. *We affirm an educational style that is committed to
personal growth and social change toward the end of full
humanity for all.* This commitment reflects our concern to
enable persons to change attitudes and behaviors that deny to
themselves and others the full humanity Christ offers in the
gospel. Changing personal attitudes requires a kind of
education that makes possible new perceptions of oneself and
world and an enlarged vision of the demands of the gospel.
Such change often takes place as persons engage in action,
individual or corporate, that calls forth new behaviors.

This commitment to work toward full humanity for all
involves change in corporate structures as well as in
individuals. Therefore, educational ministry should enable
persons to understand the systemic character of injustice in
our world and to acquire. skills of social analysis, political
functioning, and responsible use of individual and corporate
power.

10. *We affirm an educational style that, in faithfulness to
the gospel, is willing to enter into controversy and deal with
conflict.* Educational ministries that are concerned with
personal and social issues and that take into account the
different values and lifestyles that exist within the Christian
community and in the culture will inevitably become involved
in conflict. Educational programs that deal with the real
world and the life situation of people will often challenge the
vested interests of given individuals and groups or threaten
time-honored understandings of meaning and value.
Education must be willing to run this risk and find ways to
overcome resulting conflict in a context of mutual respect.
Significant education in the church involves dealing with
issues honestly and with passion, but also dealing with
persons with understanding and compassion.

11. *We are committed to experimentation and innovation
in pursuit of educational excellence.* The ineffectiveness of
many current educational programs, the challenge of a
rapidly changing cultural and world situation, and the need
for a continuing reformation of church and society, demand
that we place a high premium on experimentation and
creative innovation. Developing, trying out, and evaluating
new ways of doing education, different ways of fitting
together the elements of educational design, and new

arrangements of responsibility among local, area, and national bodies are all essential.

12. *We affirm a partnership style of planning and implementing.* Persons and agencies need to plan in partnership with those for whom any potential program is being developed. This style implies collegiality among the staffs of national boards, regional agencies and judicatories, and congregations or other structures.

13. *We affirm an open, flexible style that recognizes diversity in programs and stances.* A great diversity of theological, sociological, and educational assumptions exists within the total constituency of JED. We intend to maintain a broad stance and an open style that will not inhibit segments of the constituency from pursuing their educational mission in divergent ways from a broadly interpreted theological base.

We also affirm a variety of educational models, programs, and resources in the educational programs of local churches, groups of churches, and paracongregational institutions, by themselves or in cooperation with secular institutions. The future will require more flexible scheduling, more diverse groupings of learners, more varied settings and methodologies for teaching-learning experiences, and use of a variety of media as tools of exploration and expression.

14. *We are committed to a professionally competent educational ministry.* The guidance of personnel trained in Christian education will be important in helping the Christian community in its various manifestations to analyze situations, establish goals, and plan, implement, and evaluate educational programs. This does not imply a domination of educational ministries by professionals, since this commitment is linked with a commitment to partnership with those involved in the programs under consideration. It does call for a new competence and breadth of vision in educational leadership.

Constituency

The constituency for the educational ministries of the church includes all those who are related to the Christian community and all those in the general public who can be reached by the church. But for purposes of planning programs and strategies it is essential to identify particular constituencies that need attention. The following constituencies are overlapping, and they are not meant to represent program groupings, although some programs and strategies may be planned specifically for these groups.

1. *The Christian Community has responsibility in relation to persons who have been particularly victimized by society or are in special personal need.* Our faith story is of a God who acts for human liberation, who stands with the oppressed, the poor, the outcast, the handicapped, the sick. The Christian community is called, therefore, to give particular attention in its educational and other ministries to such persons and groups. We are called as Christians to be advocates of powerless and oppressed peoples in our own society and around the world. This includes all those who have been victimized by racial and economic injustice, by political oppression, or who have been entrapped by social structures or by stereotyped cultural roles. The church's advocacy in relation to these people involves entering into the depths of their situation, alleviating the immediate effects of it wherever possible, and joining them in their particular struggles for justice and in the common struggle for liberation and justice in the world.

The Christian community must be a caring community, not only in relation to social injustice and oppression, but also in relation to individuals. This means that in its educational and other ministries the church meets special needs and reaches out to people in times of personal crisis.

2. *The Christian community includes people of all ages.* Its ministry to its different age-group constituencies must take account of the developmental processes and the particular life situations of children, youth, and adults in today's world.

a. *Children.* During the childhood years basic feelings about self, others, and the world are established; and although these feelings are subject to modification, those established in early childhood tend to have lifelong consequences. The childhood years are years of rapid growth and of great quantities of learning.

The ministry of the Christian community with children includes concern for their whole development--their health and welfare as well as their growth in the Christian faith. Hence its ministry is one of advocacy as well as education. The church's educational ministry in relation to children is largely that of affirming their personhood, including them in the life of the community, and sharing with them the story, the ethos, and the values of the Christian faith. The education of children in the church should enhance their freedom and capability as thinking, decision-making persons, in part through involving them in the life, decision-making, and action of the whole congregation, as well as providing educational experiences with their own peers.

b. *Youth.* The youth and young adult years are a time of rapid growth and change and of making critical decisions about one's identity, vocation, and commitments. Persons under thirty are among the major groups shaping the values of society. Many young people today are caught up in a search for meaning and personal affirmation. Some of these espouse a mystical, personalistic, anti-organizational individualism and some are attracted to charismatic movements. Others relate themselves to social movements that radically criticize present-day society and work for change.

The ministry of the Christian community with youth must take with utmost seriousness the particular crises of the age group and provide a supportive community in which young people can wrestle with their own crucial life issues. Young people must be full participants in the life and mission of the church and included in its decision-making structures. The church's ministry with youth must be open-ended and dialogic. It must be supportive of young people's efforts to be responsibly engaged in interpreting the meanings of the Christian faith and in shaping the future of their own lives, the Christian community, and the world.

c. *Adults.* Through the adult years persistent life issues of identity, vocation, responsibility, and meaning do not lessen in urgency, although they often appear to do so because most adults acquire more or less stablilized patterns of coping with them. But these patterns are often disrupted as personal crises and rapid social change present new demands. As this happens, values have to be reevaluated, meanings reconceptualized, and new decisions made. The adult years bring heavy responsibility in relation to occupation and earning a living, in relation to family and friends (including the special responsibility of child-rearing carried by many during at least part of their adult years), and in relation to church, community, and the body politic. These responsibilities can be sources of fulfillment, perplexity, self-doubt and, for some, despair.

The ministry of the Christian community with adults is one of providing both sustenance and challenge. The church must be a community within which adults tell and hear the story of faith and work through the new situations, personal and social, in which they find themselves. The Christian community should enable people to wrestle with a wide range of ethical issues and with the meaning of human life. At the same time, the Christian community must challenge its adult constituency to be active shapers of the present and future social order.

d. *Older Adults*. For many older adults, retirement brings new opportunities to engage in pursuits that had to be set aside during their working years. This means that they can participate more vigorously than before in the life of the Christian community. Freed from responsibilities of earlier years and from ties with the established order of things, some older adults are ready for new perceptions of themselves and their world. They may be ready to see new visions and to help shape a new world. Other older adults, however, facing failing health and greatly lessening energy, have to curtail activity and may have to struggle with questions about their own usefulness and personal worth. Many have to struggle with problems of limited, fixed income. All older adults face an identity crisis as retirement and changing roles and responsibilities present new problems and questions. They also face loneliness as death comes to friends and relatives or as their own lack of mobility shrinks their circle of companions.

The ministry of the Christian community with older adults must include challenge, nurture, and support. Varieties of opportunities should be available for older adults to participate in the Christian Community and to give leadership to the full extent of their abilities and energy. Opportunities should also be offered for their continuing nurture in the faith, enabling them to reflect upon life's meanings, sort out values, and bring their faith perspectives to bear on their own personal situations and the world in which they live. The Christian community also has a special role in being the support community that stands by the elderly in times of loneliness and distress, sickness and death.

3. *The Christian community ministers to certain constituencies in relation to their particular roles and responsibilities.*

a. *Parents and parent-surrogates.* Because of the importance of the childhood and youth years, the Christian community has a special ministry with parents an parent-surrogates. This ministry includes being a support community for parents and providing educational opportunities for them that deal with the psychosocial development of children and youth and the appropriate roles for adults, home, and society to play in fostering full development.

This ministry to parents and parent-surrogates is not limited to those who are within the Christian community. The church is called to reach out beyond its own membership to work with parents in the community, with other concerned persons, with other voluntary associations, and with public agencies to improve the services available to parents and to protect the rights and welfare of the young.

b. *Single Persons.* The church is called to respond to the reality of the growing number of single persons in a couples-oriented society. Single persons, particularly divorced and widowed, are often treated like minority persons, so that frequently they become a hurting people who are the victims of stereotyping and oppression. The church's ministry should affirm singlehood as a natural and happy lifestyle and should seek to enable single persons to live creative and fulfilling lives. This ministry should reaffirm that single persons are people with intellectual, emotional, and spiritual resources to contribute to the life of the church and society.

c. *All those in leadership roles in the church.* Whenever the Christian community calls its members to take leadership responsibilities on its behalf, it also takes on responsibility to support these leaders and provide appropriate means for them to equip themselves for their tasks. This principle applies to the full range of leadership roles--elders, deacons, teachers, committee members, advisors to youth or other groups, trustees, choir members.

Much of the needed equipping and training can be done on the job, but special training opportunities tailored to particular needs should also be provided.

In this day when time pressures bear in upon people, the expectations that members of the Christian community have of one another should be high but also realistic, with terms of office and the nature of the responsibility clearly established and much support and encouragement given.

d. *Professional leadership of the church, lay and clergy.* The ability of the church to be faithful to its heritage and mission and to engage in shaping the future depends in considerable measure on the continuing education of its professional leadership.

New styles of leadership, less dependent upon the authority traditionally conferred on the ordained, must be developed. - Leaders will need to be in tune with the demand by youth, laymen, and laywomen for shared leadership. Functional competence and personal capacity seem to be more effective than structural authority in bringing the specialized knowledge and skills of the professional into the service of the Christian community.

e. *Shapers of values and social structures.* Within the membership of the Christian community and within the scope of its influence are many persons who exercise particular power in shaping cultural values and the structures of society. The church should enter into dialogue with these people, bearing witness to the ethical dimensions of social issues, to a vision of justice and world community and, as appropriate, to the faith community's perceptions of God's mission and to our Christian calling to faithfulness in that mission.

These and other constituency groups should be dealt with in their particularity, but always within the context of the whole inhabited earth and the common destiny which we share and must help to shape.

The JED partnership in its particular calling in educational ministry shares the calling of the whole people of God to be shapers of the future in faithfulness to God's design, as best we can discern it. So we enter the future, assured that the saving work of the Lord of history continues in our midst and that we are called to participate in it.

* * * * * * * * * *

Princeton's M.A. Syllabus
(1983)

[From *A Syllabus For Candidates for the Degree of Master of Arts, Preparatory for the Professional Examination* (Princeton, New Jersey: Princeton Theological Seminary, 1983), pp. 1-10.]

INTRODUCTION

A professional examination means one that tests the ability of the student to derive, defend, and apply basic and essential principles in carrying on the teaching ministry of the church. The student is thus examined on knowledge in the foundational and practical areas of Christian education (including Biblical studies, history, theology, the behavioral disciplines; and theory, curriculum, method and administration of Christian education). The examination also covers how this knowledge of the foundation areas is put together in terms of basic and essential principles that may guide in conducting the operational aspects of Christian education. Further, the use of these principles in planning, conducting, and evaluating Christian education in representative situations is considered.

The professional examination is six hours in length, divided into four one-and-a-half hour periods as follows:

1. Theory (focusing upon practical theology and Christian education theory and involving Biblical studies, history, theology, and the educational disciplines).

2. Method (focusing on teaching and group leadership and involving the theological and educational disciplines).

3. Curriculum (focusing on teaching and group leadership and involving the Biblical, historical, theological, and educational disciplines).

4. Administration (focusing on the area of administration of Christian education and involving the historical, theological, and educational disciplines).

The professional examination, of course, is only a check on more fundamental matters. These more fundamental matters are the mastery of the theological, behavioral, and educational disciplines that are foundational to Christian education; the hammering out of a point of view that is theoretically sound and supportable and at the same time functional and dependable in practice; and training in the skills and habits of thought and action that spell truly effective professional operation.

Central emphasis on the theoretical side is placed upon the working out of a conceptual framework for Christian education, rooted in the theological, behavioral, and educational disciplines. This syllabus is intended as a guide by which this may be begun and brought to a point of reasonable competence.

A conceptual framework for Christian education draws upon and seeks to organize vast, complicated, and somewhat recalcitrant fields of knowledge and experience. In spite of the difficulties, competent Christian educators can and must make the attempt to work out such a conceptual framework to serve as a basic orientation and guide for their work. To accomplish this end, this syllabus proposes: (1) a central concept that may serve to organize the entire field, and (2) certain primary, original, and advanced materials in the various fields.

The central organizing concept is intended as a thread of meaning by which the fields may be held together and as a major category of inquiry by which the Christian educator's study may be focused.

The central concept that may serve to organize the entire field for the Christian educator is the concept of revelation -- the reality, power, judgment, and love of God, so given that humanity is reconciled and enabled to respond appropriately.

The concept of revelation can bring the disciplines of the college or university into~focus for the Christian educator.

The liberal arts and the sciences are the most advanced and useful ways we know of grasping our world, organizing our experience, and mining for meaning and new truth. Revelation--for self-disclosure of God and his seeking love in Jesus Christ--provides a new setting for understanding and using the liberal arts and the sciences. This new setting is both liberating and corrective; liberating, in that it provides a perspective from which one may evaluate these studies; and corrective, in that it will not permit these studies to be exhaustive. Understood in this way, the central concept of revelation allows Christian educators to peruse, weigh, and use the behavioral and educational disciplines with integrity.

At the same time, the concept of revelation is the Christian educator's clue to the theological disciplines. The theological curriculum consists of Biblical studies, history, theology, and practical theology. Each is an attempt to get at some fundamental aspect of revelation. Biblical studies are set up to identify, analyze, and interpret the sources of the knowledge of revelation. History is the study that traces the modes and means of response to revelation through the years. Theology is the discipline that discusses and interprets the meaning of revelation. Practical theology's task is to suggest appropriate modes and means of response to revelation. Christian education is a discipline within practical theology whose objective is "to help persons to be aware of God's self-disclosure and seeking love in Jesus Christ and to respond in faith and love--to the end that they may know who they are and what their human situation means, grow as children of God rooted in the Christian community, live in the Spirit of God in every relationship, fulfill their common discipleship in the world, and abide in the Christian hope."

Code to abbreviations: PB - paperback; OP - out of print. Books are listed in logical thematic sequence.

BIBLICAL STUDIES

Biblical studies seek to identify, analyze and interpret the sources of the knowledge of revelation. The concern is to understand the faith and life of the believing community, Israel, from the time of its formation to the time of its re-formation and renewal through Jesus Christ. The process is theological from start to finish. We have access to the faith of the community (its testimony to God's dealing with his people) only through the study of the history of biblical traditions. The emphasis is upon the believing and worshiping community, in its various historical phases.

The work of the Biblical Department is divided into two fields, Old Testament and New Testament. These are not fundamentally separate. The Church lives by its relation to both. There are important aspects of the work of the Biblical Department that are common to the Old and New Testaments, or in which the work of the former is intended to feed into the latter.

A.   *The Oxford Annotated Bible With the Apocrypha*, Expanded Edition (Oxford University Press, 1977).

B.   The Old Testament:
von Rad, Gerhard, *Old Testament Theology*

Vol. I.   *The Theology of Israel's Historical Traditions* (Harper and Row, 1962).

Vol. II.   *The Theology of Israel's Prophetic Traditions* (Harper and Row, 1965).

Bright, John, *History of Israel* (Westminster, 1972).

Anderson, Bernhard, *Understanding the Old Testament* (Prentice Hall, 1966).

C.   The New Testament:
Jeremias, Joachim, *New Testament Theology: The Proclamation of Jesus* (Scribners, 1971).

Kee, Howard Clark, Franklin W. Young, and Karlfried Froehlich, *Understanding the New Testament* (Prentice- Hall, 1973).

Jeremias, Joachim, *The Parables of Jesus*, revised edition (Scribner's, 1963).

Bornkamm, Gunther, *Paul*, (Harper & Row, 1971).

HISTORY

History traces the modes and means of response to revelation through the years. Its obvious relevance, however, is to the present. Its purpose is to illuminate the present and assist in planning for the future by the analysis and interpretation of the events of the past. For this reason the disciplines of church history, history of religions, sociology of religion, and ecumenics are included within the study of history. These fields find a bond of union in their common historical and social approach to the study of religion from within the context of the Christian faith. From this perspective all alike emphasize process and movement in religion; and all alike emphasize the interaction between religion and its environment. The History of Religions examines the various ideological and structural forms which humanity's search for ultimate reality and commitment has assumed, and the changes through which these forms have passed as the result of interaction with other types of human experience. Christianity and Society brings to bear upon the study of religion the resources of the behavioral sciences. Church History seeks to give theological understandings of the events, ideas, and institutions of the Christian past. Ecumenics is concerned with the Christian church's mission and unity in the modern world.

A. *Church History*

In the early centuries of the church the followers of Jesus developed a church institution with definite structure and officers, a pattern of worship, a basic statement of the faith, an ethic and disciplinary procedure to maintain it, missionary tactics, a canon of authoritative writings. Every one of these functions of the Christian movement has experienced a varying history from that day to this.

In addition, the church has been variously involved with the states of many centuries, with several philosophical and scientific systems, with a series of artistic and literary styles, with diverse orders of economic life, and with an increasing number of non-Christian religions or philosophies of life. Each of these types of relations can be illuminated by a long historical perspective.

It is possible, however, to make valid generalizations about great epochs with enduring structures, such as the church in

the pagan Roman Empire, or the Christian Empire after
Constantine, the church of the Byzantine middle ages, or of
the Latin West, the crisis of the Reformation with its
consequences, and the secularization of modern Western
civilization. Within these epochs, the various functions and
relations of the church have formed in each case a distinctive
configuration of polarities.

The dynamics of the historical process are also significant,
as religious, technological, social and political factors
interplay in changing proportions to affect the life of the
Christian community.   Historical "causation" or agency is
perennially fascinating.

Concreteness and human color are given to these abstract
relations   and   functions   by   studying   biographically
representative   administrators,   theologians,   preachers,
reformers, missionaries, saints and martyrs, and various
categories of lay Christians.

The student should endeavor to reorganize and interpret
these materials along the lines of such themes as those
suggested above, often cutting across chronological and
geographical lines.   It is capacity to use and interpret
historical information that evidences command of the subject.
Such   command   consists   in   the   marriage   of   precise
information with interpretive perspective.

Hudson, Winthrop, *Religion in America* (PB -
Scribner, 1965).

Bainton, Roland, *Christendom* (PB - Harper and
Row Torchbook, 1966).

B. *History of Religions*

The student is expected to have an understanding of the
history of religions and the phenomenology of religion. Such
an understanding is needed for the study of religion in depth
as well as for interfaith and intercultural communication.

Ling, Trevor, *A History of Religion East and
West: An Introduction and Interpretation.* (PB - Harper and
Row, 1968).

Smart, Ninian, *The Phenomenon of Religion*
(Seabury Press, 1973).

C. *Christianity and Society*

The areas of concern in Christianity and society are a
human science understanding of religion and religious
organization, as well as problems of justice and peace.

Baum, Gregory, *Religion and Alienation* (PB - Paulist Press, 1975).

Weber, Max, *The Sociology of Religion* (PB - Beacon Press, 1963).

D. *Ecumenics*

Ecumenics is concerned with the strategy and relations of the church as a world missionary community. This includes study of the biblical and theological foundations of the Christian mission and of the contemporary human situation; the urgent need for renewal in the life of the Church if it is to be a missionary community in the modern world; questions of missionary strategy; and the history and present developments in the ecumenical movement.

Newbigin, Leslie, *The Open Secret* (Eerdmans, 1978).

THEOLOGY

Theology itself discusses and interprets the meaning of revelation. Sharply critical and painstakingly constructive, it is concerned with the method and substance for expressing the faith. The four areas of investigation with which theology proper is concerned are as follows:

A. *History of Doctrine*

The history of doctrine is a discipline in the modern church in close relation to critical historical studies in other fields. The student is to know the history of the discipline and the general outline of the development of doctrine from the beginning and should be familiar with the problems that dominated each period both in terms of the major theologians and the various official doctrinal standards.

Bettenson, Henry, *Documents of the Christian Church* (Second edition) (Oxford University Press, 1963).

Leith, John H., *Creeds of the Churches* (PB - Doubleday Anchor Books, 1963).

Lohse, Bernhard, *A Short History of Christian Doctrine* (Fortress, 1966).

B. *Doctrinal Theology*

Systematic theology is concerned with the clarification, definition, and interpretation of the Christian faith. It takes two forms: (1) comprehensive treatments of the wholebody of doctrine, and (2) studies of specific doctrines.

The Book of Confessions (PB - Office of the General Assembly, UPCUSA, 2nd edition, 1970, PB).

Macquarrie, John, *Principles of Christian Theology*, 2nd edition (Scribners, 1977, PB).

Barth, Karl, *Dogmatics in Outline* (Harper and Row, 1969, PB)

Barth, Karl, *The Humanity of God* (John Knox, 1970, PB).

Cobb, John and David Griffin, *Process Theology* (Westminster, 1976, PB).

McBrien, Richard, *Catholicism* (one-volume study edition, Winston, 1981, PB).

Dulles, Avery, *Models of the Church* (Doubleday, 1974, PB).

Cone, James, *God of the Oppressed* (Seabury, 1974, PB).

Norris, Richard, *Understanding the Faith of the Church* (Seabury, 1979, PB).

McFague, Sally, *Metaphorical Theology* (Fortress, 1982).

C. *Christian Ethics*

The distinction between systematic theology and Christian ethics is important for purposes of study, although in life Christian faith and obedience are inseparable. Christian ethics is the effort to discover the truth of the Christian faith in the context of human life and action amid the problems of the world.

Barth, Karl, *Church Dogmatics* Vol. II, Part IV. (T. and T. Clark, 1981).

Beach, Waldo and H. Richard Niebuhr (eds.), *Christian Ethics* (Ronald Press Co., 1955).

Boesak, Allan, *Farewell to Innocence* (Orbis, 1977).

Bonhoeffer, Dietrich, *Ethics* (PB - Macmillan, 1955).

Gustafson, James M., *Christ and the Moral Life* (Harper and Row, 1968).

Lehmann, Paul, *Ethics in a Christian Context* (Harper and Row, 1963).

D. *Philosophy of Religion*

Philosophy and theology, although distinct in many ways and often bitterly antagonistic, share a venerable tradition of close relationship and mutual concern. The philosophy of the classical Greek tradition (Plato, Aristotle) and of more modern times (Kant, Hegel) have exerted substantial influence upon all phases of Western thought including theology. Today philosophy in its existential forms (Kierkegaard, Heidegger) or as linguistic analysis (Wittgenstein, the "Oxford" school) is particularly concerned to test the meaning of religious language, statements about faith, and propositions of theological truth.

Armstrong, A. H. and R. A. Marcus, *Christian Faith and Greek Philosophy* (Sheed and Ward, 1964); or Hatch, E., *The Influence of Greek Ideas on Christianity* (Peter Smith; and Harper and Row, 1957, PB); or Shiel, J., *Greek Thought and the Rise of Christianity* (Longmans, 1968).

Hick, John, *Classical and Contemporary Readings in the Philosophy of Religion*, 2nd edition (Prentice-Hall, 1970).

Hick, John, *Philosophy of Religion*, 3rd edition (Prentice-Hall, 1983, PB).

- As a companion piece to guide readings in the previous volume.

THE EDUCATIONAL DISCIPLINES

The Christian educator brings insight from the perspective of the disciplines that deal with revelation to bear upon the educational concerns that are illuminated by philosophy, history, psychology, sociology, and educational theory and practice.

A. *Philosophy and History of Education*

The first group of readings is intended to put education in as deep and broad a perspective as possible. The last three readings in Section I are primary sources in recent philosophy of education.

I. Morris, Van Cleve and Paul Pai, *Philosophy and the American School* (Houghton Mifflin, 1976).

Dewey, John, *Democracy and Education* (Macmillan, 1916) (PB available)

Whitehead, Alfred N., *The Aims of Education and Other Essays* (PB - Macmillan Co., 1929).

Green, Thomas F., *The Activities of Teaching* (McGraw-Hill, 1971).

Phenix, Philip, *Realms of Meaning* (McGraw-Hill, 1971).

II.   Power, Edward J., *Main Currents in the History of Education* (McGraw-Hill, 1970).

Brauner, Charles J., *American Educational Theory* (OP-Prentice-Hall, 1964).

Mason, Robert E., *Contemporary Educational Theory* (PB -David McKay, 1972).

Tyack, David, and Elisabeth Hansot, *Managers of Virtue, Public School Leadership in America, 1820-1980* (Basic Books, 1982).

Cramer, J. F., and G. 5. Brown, *Contemporary Education* (Harcourt, Brace & World, 1965).

B. *Behavioral Studies and Education*

The books in this section deal with personality theory, developmental theory, learning, creativity, sociology, and social psychology.

Hall, Calvin, and Gardner Lindzey, *Theories of Personality* (Wiley, 1970).

Brusselmans, Christiane, *Toward Moral and Religious Maturity* (The First International Conference on Moral and Religious Development) Convened by Christiane Brusselmans (PB - Silver Burdett, 1980).

Elkind, David, *The Child's Reality* (Erlbaum Assoc., 1978).

Erikson, Erik, *Childhood and Society* (Second Edition) (Norton, 1964) (PB available)

Flavell, John H., *The Developmental Psychology of Jean Piaget* (Van Nostrand, 1963).

Fowler, James W., *Stages of Faith, The Psychology of Human Development and the Quest for Meaning* (Harper & Row,1981).

Loder, James E., *The Transforming Moment; Understanding Convictional Experiences* (Harper & Row, 1981).

Rizzuto, Ana-Maria, *The Birth of the Living God* (University of Chicago Press, 1979).

Hilgard, Ernest R. (ed.), *Theories of Learning and Instruction* (University of Chicago Press, 1974).

Arieti, Silvano, *Creativity: The Magic Synthesis* (Basic Books, 1976).

Berger, Peter L. and Thomas Luckman, *The Social Construction of Reality* (PB - Doubleday, 1966).

Havighurst, Robert J. and Bernice L. Neugarten, *Society and Education* (Allyn and Bacon, Inc., 1967).

Bar-Tal, Daniel and Leonard Sake, *Social Psychology of Education* (Hemisphere, 1978).

Batson, C. Daniel and W. Larry Ventis, *The Religious Experience, A Social-Psychological Perspective* (Oxford U. Press, 1982).

Brown, Robert, *Social Psychology* (Free Press, 1965).

C. *Educational Practice*

Representative studies of the application of behavioral and social research findings to educational practice are included in this list.

Bruner, Jerome 5., *The Process of Education* (PB - Vintage, Books, 1960).

Rogers, Carl R., *Freedom to Learn* (Charles E. Merrill, 1969), (PB available)

Freire, Paulo, *Pedagogy of the Oppressed* (PB - Seabury, 1970).

Reimer, Everett, *School is Dead: Alternatives in Education* (Doubleday, 1971)

Goldhammer, Robert, *Clinical Supervision* (Holt, Rinehard and Winston, 1969).

Kemp, C. Gratton, *Small Groups for Self-Renewal* (Seabury Press, 1971).

Zaltman, Gerald and Robert Duncan, *Strategies for Planned Change* (Wiley Interscience, 1977).

D. *Periodicals*

> *Educational Theory*
> *The Harvard Educational Review*
> *The Teachers College Record*

PRACTICAL THEOLOGY

Practical Theology's task is to suggest appropriate modes and means of response to revelation. Its areas include worship, preaching, education, pastoral theology, and administration.

Getz, Gene A., *Sharpening the Focus of the Church* (PB -Moody Press, 1974).

Hiltner, Seward, *Preface to Pastoral Theology* (PB -Abingdon Press, 1958).

Church polity is to be seen in its theological context. Appropriate denominational guides should be carefully studied.

For the additional practical fields, the student is referred to:

Faber, Heije, *Psychology of Religion* (Westminster, 1975).

Hendrick, John R., *Opening the Door of Faith* (PB - John Knox, 1977).

MacLeod, Donald, *Presbyterian Worship* (PB - John Knox, 1956).

White, James F., *Introduction to Christian Worship* (PB - Abingdon, 1980).

Clinebell, Howard, *Basic Types of Pastoral Counseling* (Abingdon, 1966).

Durka, Gloria and Joanmarie Smith (eds.), *Aesthetic Dimensions of Religious Education* (PB - Paulist Press, 1979).

Durka, Gloria and Joanmarie Smith (eds.) *Family Ministry* (PB - Winston Press, 1980).

CHRISTIAN EDUCATION

Within practical theology, Christian education's concerns are for sound and adequate theory and dependable practice in method, curriculum, and administration.

A. Theory

Christian education theory may be understood best when viewed historically, with special attention to the religious education movement, the reaction to that movement, and the varieties of viewpoints that have emerged since.

a. Historical Backgrounds

For the history of ideas in religious education see:

Rood, Wayne R., *Understanding Christian Education* (OP - Abingdon, 1970).

The arrangement of the list of books on historical background is generally chronological. These books are supplementary to, and to be read against the background of, the readings in the history of education and church history (see above).

Muirhead, Ian A., *Education in the New Testament* (PB - Association Press, 1975).

Worley, Robert C., *Preaching and Teaching in the Earliest Church* (Westminster, 1962).

Sherrill, Lewis Joseph, *The Rise of Christian Education* (Macmillan, 1944).

Towns, Elmer L. (ed.), *A History of Religious Educators* (Baker Book House, 1975).

Henderson, Robert W., *The Teaching Office in the Reformed Tradition* (Westminster, 1962).

Bushnell, Horace, *Christian Nurture* - Introduction by John Mulder (PB - Baker Book House, 1979).

Laqueur, Thomas Walter, *Religion and Respectability, Sunday Schools and Working Class Culture* (Yale University Press, 1976).

Little, Sara, *The Role of the Bible in Contemporary Christian Education* (OP - John Knox, 1980).

Lynn, Robert W., and Elliot Wright, *The Big Little School* (PB - Religious Education Press, 1980).

Coe, George Albert, *A Social Theory of Religious Education* (OP - Scribners, 1917).

Piveteau, Didier-Jacques, and J. T. Dillon, *Resurgence of Religious Instruction* (PB - Religious Education Press, 1977).

Boys, Mary C., *Biblical Interpretation in Religious Education* (PB - Religious Education Press, 1980).

b. Selected Contemporary Views

Not all contemporary views are represented here, but enough to present the issues under discussion in the last few years, and to indicate the flavor of that discussion. With them, the student may be drawn into the debate as it is now carried on.

Dykstra, Craig, *Vision and Character: A Christian Educator's Alternative to Kohlberg* (PB - Paulist Press, 1981).

Groome, Thomas, *Christian Religious Education* (PB - Harper and Row, 1980).

Heckman, Shirley, *On the Wings of a Butterfly* (PB - Brethren Press, 1981).

Hessel, Dieter T., *Social Ministry* (PB - Westminster Press, 1982).

Kelsey, Morton, *Can Christians Be Educated?* (PB -Religious Education Press, 1977).

Miller, Donald E., *The Wing-Footed Wanderer, Conscience and Transcendence* (Abingdon, 1977).

Moran, Gabriel, *Interplay: A Theory of Religion and Education* (St. Mary's Press, 1981).

O'Hare, Padraic (ed.), *Foundations of Religious Education* (PB - Paulist Press, 1978).

Munsey Barbara (ed.), *Moral Development, Moral Education and Kohlberg* (Religious Education Press, 1980).

Richards, Lawrence, *A Theology of Christian Education* (Zondervan, 1972).

Rummery, R. M., *Catechesis and Religious Education in a Pluralistic Society* (Our Sunday Visitor, 1976).

Russell, Letty M., *Growth in Partnership* (PB - Westminster Press, 1981).

Schaefer, James R., *Program Planning for Adult Christian Education* (PB - Newman Press, 1972).

Seymour, Jack L. and Donald E. Miller (eds.), *Contemporary Approaches to Christian Education* (PB - Abingdon, 1982).

Westerhoff, John H., III and Gwen Kennedy Neville, *Generation to Generation* (Pilgrim Press, 1974).

B. *Method*

Method in Christian education does not consist fundamentally of specific ways of doing things, but rather in basic decisions as to the ways in which the elements in the field of relationships interact educationally. The books listed are representative of some of the disciplines and schools of thought that are contributing to the discussion on method at this level.

Boehlke, Robert R., *Theories of Learning in Christian Education* (Westminster, 1961).

Joyce, Bruce and Marshal Weil, *Models of Teaching* (Prentice-Hall, 1980).

Rood, Wayne R., *The Art of Teaching Christianity* (PB -Abingdon, 1968).

Torrance, Thomas F., *The School of Faith* (Harper and Row, 1959).

Clark, Dorothy, *Teach Me, Please Teach Me* (David C. Cook, 1974).

Muller, Farenholz, Geiko (ed.), *Partners in Life: The Handicapped and The Church* (PB - World Council of Churches, 1980).

C. *Curriculum*

Curriculum is the plan by which the church undertakes systematically to fulfill its teaching responsibility.

Gress, James R. (ed.) and David Purpel *Curriculum,_An Introduction to the Field* (McCutchan Publishing, 1978).

Wyckoff, D. Campbell, *Theory and Design of Christian Education Curriculum* (Westminster, 1961).

Colson, Howard and Raymond Rigdon, *Understanding Your Church's Curriculum* (PB - Broadman, 1981).

D. *Administration*

Religious education leans on secular theory and practice.

Griffiths, Daniel E., *Administrative Theory* (PB - Appleton-Century-Crofts, 1959).

Bower, Robert K., *Administering Christian Education* (PB -Eerdmans, 1964).

Campbell, Thomas C. and Gary B. Reierson, *The Gift of Administration* (Westminster Press, 1981, PB)

Downs, Thomas, *The Parish As Learning Community* (PB - Paulist Press, 1970).

Harris, Maria (ed.), *Parish Religious Education* (PB - Paulist Press, 1978).

Wyckoff, D. Campbell, *How to Evaluate Your Christian Education Program* (Westminster, 1962).

Bausch, William J., *Traditions, Tensions, Transitions in Ministry* (Twenty-Third Publications, 1982).

Bossart, Donald, *Creative Conflict in Religious Education and Church Administration* (Religious Education Press, 1980).

Gangel, Kenneth 0., *Building Leaders for Church Education* (Moody Press, 1981).

Keating, Charles J., *The Leadership Book* (revised edition) (PB - Paulist Press, 1982).

Lee, Harris W., *Theology of Administration* (Augsburg Publishing House, 1981).

Judy Marvin, *The Multiple Staff Ministry* (Abingdon, 1969).

Mitchell, Kenneth, *Psychological and Theological Relationships in the Multiple Staff Ministry* (Westminster, 1966).

Furnish, Dorothy, *DRE/DCE - The History of a Profession* (UMC, 1976) or Harris, Maria, *The D.R.E. Book* (PB -Paulist Press, 1976).

E. *Religion and Education*

Questions of religion and education (public, private, higher, and ecumenical) are dealt with in the following:

Lumen Vitae (Roman Catholic, but including Protestant interests; scholarly).

The Living Light: An Interdisciplinary Review of Christian Education (official publication of the Department of Education of the United States Catholic Conference).

Journal of Religious Education (Scripture Press Foundation, scholarly).

SUPPLEMENT TO SYLLABUS: ROMAN CATHOLIC CANDIDATES

Roman Catholic candidates are, in general, responsible for all of the requirements mentioned in the syllabus; they will need to pass the professional examination explained on page 1 of the syllabus and to acquire the broad perspectives and knowledge through reading and course-work as detailed throughout the entire syllabus. In addition, Roman Catholic candidates, because of their training for positions of leadership in the Roman Catholic tradition, will need to offer evidence of their understanding of official catechetical documents as well as major Roman Catholic catechists represented in other sections of this syllabus. The following official Roman Catholic catechetical documents are suggested:

Documents of Vatican II, Walter Abbott, S.J., (ed.) (American Press, 1964).

Sharing the Light of Faith: The National Catechetical Directory for Catholics of the United States (United States Catholic Conference, 1978).

To Teach as Jesus Did (United States Catholic Conference, 1972).

Justice in the World (United States Catholic Conference, 1972).

Rite of Christian Initiation of Adults (United States Catholic Conference, 1974).

Dr. Doris Donnelly serves as Faculty Adviser for Roman Catholic students.

Notes

[1] For a splendid summary of this matter, see <u>The Seven Liberal Arts in the Middle Ages</u>, ed. David L. Wagner (Bloomington: Indiana University Press, 1983), pp. 2ff.

Index

A

Abraham, 27
administration, 130, 144, 160, 205, 206, 216, 217
America, 1, 17, 51, 128, 149, 153, 189, 190, 210, 214
Aquinas, St. Thomas, 119
arithmetic, 4, 6, 167
astronomy, 4, 6, 7, 8, 167
atonement, 69, 132, 138
Aubrey, Edwin E., 92
authoritarian, 78, 82

B

Bower, William Clayton, 49, 60, 96, 87, 221
Buber, Martin, 172, 179
Bushnell, Horace, 17, 18, 27, 35, 47, 49, 106, 218

C

catechetical, 98, 222
ceremonials, 78
Chave, Ernest, 49, 66
community, 169, 191, 192, 193, 194, 195, 196, 197, 198, 199, 200, 201, 202, 203, 204, 207, 208, 210, 211
community, 38, 39, 83, 84, 92, 93, 96, 97, 110, 114, 115, 116, 117, 118, 119, 120, 121, 122, 123, 124, 125, 126, 127, 128, 129, 145, 146, 147, 148, 151, 152, 153, 154, 159, 160, 161, 162
congregation, 7, 103, 145, 146, 147, 148, 149, 150, 151, 152, 153, 154, 155, 156, 157, 159, 161, 162, 163, 194, 201
Corinthians, 151, 159
creed, 100, 102, 103, 178
curriculum, 22, 49, 53, 88, 92, 101, 102, 103, 107, 130, 144, 147, 163, 167, 168, 169, 170, 173, 174, 176, 179, 181, 182, 185, 186, 205, 207, 217

D

Darwin, Charles, 17, 18, 35, 37, 47
demonic, 128, 129
Dewey, John, 37, 38, 41, 44, 47, 49, 214

E

ecclesiastical, 2, 5, 6, 53, 59, 185
Elliot, Harrison S, 218
Ellwood, Charles A., 87
enculturation model, 18
Ephesians, 106
ethics, 101, 171, 172, 173, 175, 183, 212
ethos, 18, 145, 167, 196, 201
Florovsky, George, 119, 120

G

geometry, 4, 6, 8, 167
gospel, 167, 191, 192, 194, 198
gospel, 59, 88, 125, 130, 131, 133, 134, 135, 136, 137, 139, 140, 141, 142, 143, 144
grace, 104, 122, 123, 127, 149, 177, 193

H

habits, 45, 58, 61, 108, 206

I

imagination, 41, 66, 178
indoctrination, 68, 69, 76, 101, 103, 105
injustice, 9, 28, 32, 193, 198, 200
intelligence, 24, 34, 54, 72, 103, 156, 178
interfaith, 180, 210
Isaiah, 94, 134

K

koinonia, 121, 122, 124

L

Lawrence, Brother, 174, 219
Lutherans, 154

M

maturity, 23, 74, 78, 106, 117, 141, 150, 156, 159
Maurus, Rhabanus, 1, 8, 15, 167, 168
Miller, Randolph Crump, 87, 88, 97, 219, 220

music, 4, 6, 123, 167, 171
mystical, 2, 6, 201

N

neo-orthodox, 87, 88
noesis, 172

O

oikumene, 195
omnipresence, 178, 179, 181

P

passions, 26, 129
personality, 58, 59, 62, 74, 89, 90, 103, 104, 105, 113, 157, 215
Phenix, Philip, 167, 168, 173, 214
piety, 3, 30, 34, 52
Polanyi, Michael, 172
positivist, 185
practices, 50, 68, 70, 72, 80, 81, 179
pragmatism, 37
praxis, 88
prayer, 32, 33, 77, 80, 96, 122, 124, 161
Presbyterian, 189, 190, 217
progressive-liberal movement, 49, 87, 88
prophetic, 20, 95, 126, 154, 193
providence, 77
psychology, 17, 88, 90, 105, 107, 113, 213, 215
public school, 68, 110, 162, 182, 183

R

reformation, 198, 208
relationships, 68, 71, 84, 102, 114, 115, 116, 118, 136, 137, 138, 142, 157, 168, 169, 171, 195, 197, 220
religions, 59, 179, 181, 183, 209, 210
Religious Education Association, 49
religious education, 1, 15, 17, 18, 37, 49, 54, 68, 69, 70, 72, 73, 78, 81, 82, 87, 88, 90, 92, 93, 96, 141, 145, 157, 158
revelation, 58, 60, 71, 73, 82, 123, 129, 132, 133, 137, 139, 144, 206, 207, 208, 209, 211, 213, 216
rhetoric, 4, 5, 9, 167
Richardson, Alan, 134

S

salvation, 104, 126, 135, 144
salvation, 191
salvation, 69
Santa Claus, 77
sermon, 153, 154, 155
Sherrill, Lewis Joseph, 87, 88, 114, 218
singlehood, 203
slavery, 8, 13, 135
Smith, Shelton, 87, 88, 213, 217
socialization, 91, 146, 158
Spencer, Herbert, 2, 17, 18, 20, 21, 35, 47
syllabus, 189, 206, 222
symbolics, 171, 172
synoptics, 171, 172, 173

T

Tatian, 8, 14, 15
Tillich, Paul, 179
Trent, Council of, 119

U

Unitarian Association, 50

V

Vatican II, 222
virtue, 33, 115, 123, 173, 178

W

Wittgenstein, 213
worship, 10, 54, 55, 71, 80, 100, 107, 110, 121, 122, 123, 145, 148, 149, 150, 154, 155, 162, 174, 175, 176, 177, 178, 179, 180, 181, 182, 183, 184, 186, 197, 209, 216
Wyckoff, D. Campbell, 87, 88, 129, 189, 220, 221

Ronald H. Cram received his M.A. in Christian Education and Ph.D. in Practical Theology from Princeton Theological Seminary. He is Associate Professor of Christian Education at Columbia Theological Seminary, Decatur, Georgia, and serves presently as the Executive Administrator for The Religious Education Association.